THE FUNCTION OF
THE PUBLIC SCHOOLS
IN DEALING WITH RELIGION

COMMITTEE ON RELIGION AND EDUCATION
Appointed by the American Council on Education

THE FUNCTION OF
the Public Schools
IN DEALING WITH
Religion

A REPORT ON THE EXPLORATORY STUDY
MADE BY THE COMMITTEE ON RELIGION
AND EDUCATION

AMERICAN COUNCIL ON EDUCATION
WASHINGTON D. C.

1 9 5 3

PRINTED IN THE UNITED STATES OF AMERICA

FOREWORD

THIS is the third in a series of reports, published by the American Council on Education, on the appropriate relation of religion to public education in the United States.

The first, published in 1944 under the title *Religion and Public Education* (out of print), was a summary of the principal addresses and discussions at a conference of educators convened at Princeton, New Jersey, May 12–14, 1944, by the Council in cooperation with the National Conference of Christians and Jews. This conference was an outgrowth of a suggestion made in 1939 by Dr. Herbert L. Seamans, director of the Commission on Educational Organizations of the National Conference of Christians and Jews, and of the widespread concern with the problem.

The late Dr. George F. Zook, then president of the Council, said in the Foreword to this report: "There can be no question as to the importance of the subject of the conference. Nearly all persons engaged in education in the early part of our history believed deeply that it was fundamentally wrong to eliminate religious teaching from the school program. Many are still of this same opinion. Certainly there is almost universal complaint that education has become too much a matter of learning facts and that there is altogether too little emphasis upon values and objectives. The schools and churches are therefore confronted with a common problem, but, because of the prevailing separation of church and state in this country, there is relatively little cooperation between religious organizations and the public schools. How to bring about a reconsideration of the relation of religion to education was the central theme of the conference."

The participants in the conference represented public elementary, secondary, and higher education, as well as institutions and agencies of the three major faith groups in America. In summarizing the discussions Dr. F. Ernest Johnson said: "The conference adjourned without having inspired any expectation of quick solutions to the problems brought forth. But it did inspire a mood of profound concern, of urgency and of hope." Perhaps the most significant result was the appointment by the Council of its Committee on Religion and Education to which was assigned "the task of continuing the exploratory work of this conference and formulating a further program of activity in this field."

The second report was published in 1947 under the title *The Relation of Religion to Public Education: The Basic Principles*. It was prepared by the Council's Committee on Religion and Education "as a first step in a program of studies and experimental activities." In its summary and conclusions the committee said, "We have endeavored to state the problem arising out of the secularization of American life and education. Before it can be solved, careful studies will need to be made of local community situations, of various types of experimentation now going on, of professional and lay opinion, of legal questions involved, and of the experience of other countries. It is our intention to initiate studies of this sort to the fullest extent possible. In this report we have attempted the preliminary task of stating the problem in a context of educational principles."

This third report published by the Council—the second report of the committee—was made possible by a grant from the Rockefeller Foundation and by the cooperation of many educational and religious leaders throughout the United States. Within the frame of reference set by its 1947 report, the committee has attempted to explore the desirability and feasibility of further studies and experiments designed to discover the function of the public schools in dealing with religion. This report is, therefore, a further step in carrying out the task assigned the committee.

Publication of this report by the American Council on Education should not be understood as formal endorsement of the central conclusion: "We believe the findings of this inquiry point to factual study of religion as the best solution confronting public education in dealing with religion." Surely all can agree, however, on the improbability "that significant progress will be made toward a solution until conclusive evidence is obtained regarding the desirability and feasibility" of this approach. Hence, it is to be earnestly hoped that a solution to this vital problem will eventually be found which is recognized to be consistent both with the constitutional principles of our republic and with the importance of religion in human life.

ARTHUR S. ADAMS, *President*
American Council on Education

INTRODUCTION

THREE important policy decisions were made by the Committee on Religion and Education as guides for the conduct of the exploratory study—the findings, conclusions, and recommendations of which are presented in this report.

First, the aim was defined as "An inquiry into the function of the public schools, in their own right and on their own initiative, in assisting youth to have an intelligent understanding of the historical and contemporary role of religion in human affairs."

Second, the character of the study should be "exploratory" of opinions of responsible educational and religious leaders and "illustrative" of current practice. Primary consideration should be given to the opinions of responsible educational leaders, because the initiative for, and the administration of, further studies and experiments depend in large part upon the judgments of educators concerning their desirability and feasibility in relation to actual situations. This inquiry was designed as a further step in developing a plan for such studies and experiments, should the findings warrant such undertakings.

Third, the study should be focused on the public elementary and secondary schools and on teacher education.

Because released time religious instruction and the religious education programs of denominational schools were thought to be outside the scope of this inquiry, they were not studied and, therefore, are not included in this report. Released time religious instruction is essentially an activity of the churches or religious associations, and denominational schools are in large part free from the inherent limitations of the public schools with respect to religion. These omissions imply no judgment on the part of the committee with respect to the merits of such programs, but rather emphasize the problem of public education as the basic concern of the committee. For the same reason relatively little consideration is given to practices of church-related and independent colleges and universities.

The methods employed to obtain the substantive data for this report were: conferences with educational and religious leaders; brief questionnaires submitted to selected educational leaders, and opinionnaires submitted to selected educational and religious leaders; and a survey of other studies, reports, books, policy statements, proposals, and pronouncements, particularly those of the past decade.

This report was prepared by Professor Clarence Linton and Miss Beatrice Hall, serving respectively as director and associate director of the study, under the supervision of the committee as a whole. Its preparation involved correspondence, progress reports, preliminary drafts, numerous conferences with individual members and with a subcommittee, and five meetings of the entire committee. The committee submits the document as its own report.

CONTENTS

LIST OF TABLES

CHAPTER I

A PERSISTENT UNSOLVED PROBLEM

PUBLIC education in the United States is committed by federal and state law to the general principle that sectarian religious instruction must be excluded from the curriculum. This does not mean, however, that the problem of what to do about religion in the public schools has been solved. On the contrary, there is no clear-cut understanding of what the schools should or should not do in this field.

Some people think that the schools should leave religion completely to organized religious groups and to the home. They fear that any consideration of religion in the school will result in dangerous divisions in the community because of the emotional factors with which religion is surrounded; or they believe that the public school in a democratic society cannot handle religion without violating the religious liberty of minority groups.

Many people, however, are convinced that the public school's program of general education becomes distorted and impoverished when all religious references are excluded. They fear that neglect of religion will undermine the very foundations of individual and social morality. In their opinion the Founding Fathers did not intend to exclude religion from the schools when they restrained Congress from any move toward an "establishment of religion."

In actual practice one finds many activities which are not consistent with the assumption that religion has been excluded from the public school program. For example, Bible reading is required in some states and permitted in others. The observance of certain religious holidays, such as Christmas, is characterized in nearly all schools by the use of religious subject matter, music, and religious ceremonies. Some schools, particularly those in communities which are nearly homogeneous from a religious standpoint, go much further than this in the encouragement of participation in religion by the pupils of the school.

A few schools are beginning to experiment with the factual study of religion in order that pupils may understand its role in history and in the development of values and standards in our society.

What to do about religion in the public schools is a persistent and vital problem. It will not be solved by drifting. We urge that this problem be studied carefully, with appropriate experimentation in different communities that are willing to undertake it. The solution will have far-reaching effects on the future unity and soundness of American society.

In 1947 the Committee on Religion and Education issued our first report, *The Relation of Religion to Public Education: The Basic Principles,*[1] in which we attempted to define the problem and to state the principles on which the practice of the public schools should be based. In the light of intervening developments we would perhaps modify our position in certain respects, but in general we still subscribe to the major principles which were stated at that time. Relevant conclusions from that report may be restated as follows:

1. The problem is to find a way in public education to give due recognition to the place of religion in the culture and in the convictions of our people while at the same time safeguarding the separation of church and state.

2. The separation of American public education from church control was not intended to exclude all study of religion from the school program.

3. Teaching a common core of religious beliefs in the public schools is not a satisfactory solution.

[1] Washington: American Council on Education.

4. Teaching "moral and spiritual values" cannot be regarded as an adequate substitute for an appropriate consideration of religion in the school program.

5. Teaching which opposes or denies religion is as much a violation of religious liberty as teaching which advocates or supports any particular religious belief.

6. Introducing factual study of religion will not commit the public schools to any particular religious belief.

7. The role of the school in the study of religion is distinct from, though complementary to, the role of the church.

8. The public school should stimulate the young toward a vigorous, personal reaction to the challenge of religion.

9. The public school should assist youth to have an intelligent understanding of the historical and contemporary role of religion in human affairs.

The mounting concern over the appropriate place to be given religion in public education is evidenced by the many books, articles, and other pronouncements published in the past decade, particularly since our 1947 report. Two recent policy statements of educational leaders will serve to illustrate this concern.

The Educational Policies Commission of the National Education Association of the United States and of the American Association of School Administrators published its report on *Moral and Spiritual Values in the Public Schools*[2] in 1951. The commission maintains that the public schools, in discharging their responsibility for the development of the moral and spiritual values which the American people desire their children to hold, can and should teach *about* religion.

There are differences in opinion among both educational and religious leaders about the adequacy of the commission's statement, particularly regarding its treatment of sanctions for values and ways in which it proposes that schools should

---

[2] Washington: National Education Association.

deal with religion. This emphasizes the complexity and importance of the problem. We think, however, this report by one of the most influential educational groups in the United States is highly significant both because of the position taken and particularly because it indicates the increasing awareness on the part of educators that public schools must find appropriate methods of dealing with religion.

Although a detailed critical analysis of this document might serve to refine our committee's position on the broad problem of the relationship of religion to public education, it would be somewhat irrelevant to the immediate task of reducing our committee's 1947 position to practical specifics, as suggested by the purpose of the exploratory study. The following extracts will illustrate the position taken by the commission.

The commission says,

. . . when a point about religious opinion or religious practices arises in a classroom discussion the teacher will not brush it aside with a statement that he is not allowed to discuss this matter in the public school. There can be no doubt that the American democracy is grounded in a religious tradition. While religion may not be the only source of democratic moral and spiritual values, it is surely one of the important sources. For this objective reason, if for no other, an attitude of respect toward religion should prevail in the schools. . . .

Further on, the commission states,

A democratic society grants to every citizen the right to believe as his conscience and training dictate. The public schools can and should stress the meaning of this right to their students. Properly applied, this privilege means not only freedom of belief, but respect for the beliefs of others. . . . In declaring that the public schools should not teach religion, we wish to be entirely clear that teaching against religion is equally intolerant and intolerable. The teacher of science, for example, who tells young people that religious faith is to be condemned because it is "unscientific" is taking an unprofessional advantage of their immaturity as well as exhibiting his own. . . .

Under the heading "The Public School Can and Should Teach about Religion" the commission says,

The public schools can teach objectively *about* religion without advocating or teaching any religious creed. To omit from the classroom all references to religion and the institutions of religion is to neglect an important part of American life. Knowledge about religion is essential for a full understanding of our culture, literature, art, history, and current affairs. That religious beliefs are controversial is not an adequate reason for excluding teaching about religion from the public schools. . . .

The second policy statement to which we wish to call particular attention was published in the spring of 1952 by the superintendents of schools of cities in the United States and Canada with population over 200,000 under the title *An Educational Platform for the Public Schools: Some Phases of Instructional Policy*.[3] It is our understanding that this statement is the result of discussions held during the past several years and that it is considered tentative and therefore subject to revision in the light of further study and discussion. An extract indicates the concern of this group of educational leaders with the place of religion in the development of moral and spiritual values.

The superintendents say,

. . . History reveals the belief of the American people in God. The public schools reflect this belief in high degree. We approach the basic ethical values of life through the concepts of the Fatherhood of God and the Brotherhood of Man. . . . Religious freedom and the separation of church and state are also basic in the American tradition. No government agency (including the public schools) can have any supervision, control, or jurisdiction over religion. The teaching of religion is definitely a responsibility of the home and the church. But it is a proper function of the public schools to support and reinforce the home and the church in discharging this important responsibility. The public schools are not Godless and are not materialistic. They are not sectarian. The public schools recognize

[3] Chicago, Ill.: Educational Division, Field Enterprises, Inc.

the essential place of religion in the American way of life, but they cannot endorse, nor can they favor, any particular religion or religious system.

Moral, ethical, and spiritual values are an essential element of the public school program; the schools emphasize these values and also teach the role of religion in the development of the culture. . . .

Our position with respect to the problem under study may be briefly summarized as follows:

The public school is limited, as the private institution is not, in its treatment of religion. The constitutions, statutes, and interpretations thereof in the forty-eight states, and the decisions of the Supreme Court of the United States, make it illegal for the public school to teach religion in the sense of the attempt to inculcate sectarian religious beliefs. Even if agreement could be reached among the religiously minded on a "common core" or set of basic propositions common to and acceptable to Roman Catholics, Protestants, and Jews, there would remain the nonreligious groups in the community who would maintain that their rights were violated by any attempt to inculcate general propositions embodying religious beliefs.

On the other hand, to be silent about religion may be, in effect, to make the public school an antireligious factor in the community. Silence creates the impression in the minds of the young that religion is unimportant and has nothing to contribute to the solution of the perennial and ultimate problems of human life. This negative consequence is all the more striking in a period when society is asking the public school to assume more and more responsibility for dealing with the cultural problems of growth and development.

Therefore, it is vitally important that the public school deal with religion. There are many ways in which this may be and indeed is being done. Some are good; others, in our judgment, may be dangerous to a greater or lesser degree.

All public schools, however, can provide for the factual study of religion both as an important factor in the historical and contemporary development of our culture and as a source of values and insight for great numbers of people in finding the answers to persistent personal problems of living. Religion can, and in our judgment should, be studied in the same way as the economic and political institutions and principles of our country should be studied—not as something on which the American public school must settle all arguments and say the last word, but as something which is so much a part of the American heritage and so relevant to contemporary values that it cannot be ignored.

CHAPTER II

ILLUSTRATIONS OF PRACTICE

HOW are the public elementary and secondary schools dealing with religion? How are colleges and universities preparing teachers to deal with religion in the public schools? How do these practices conform to the suggested alternative of factual study of religion and the frame of reference presented in chapter i?

Partial answers to these questions were obtained from the replies of responsible educators to the first of four questions included in the first questionnaire used in this inquiry. The educators to whom these questionnaires were submitted were selected on the basis of the positions they occupy in American education by use of the membership list of the American Council on Education, and the *Educational Directories* of the Office of Education, Federal Security Agency. All persons within categories indicated below were included. In this instance—as was true of other instruments sent to educational leaders—the selection on the basis of position insured proportional geographical representation.

The questionnaire is reproduced in full in the Appendix (see page 94). Its principal objectives were to obtain information about current practices, and to discover what educational leaders think the public schools and the colleges and universities can and should do about religion. We are concerned here with the replies to the first question only, which was as follows:

In what specific ways do the curricula and extraclass activities of your public elementary and secondary schools[1] deal with religion and

[1] "Institution" was substituted for "public elementary and secondary schools" in the form submitted to presidents of colleges and universities.

religious institutions as a part of the culture? (We are concerned with whatever is now being done or planned to assist youth to have an intelligent understanding of the historical and contemporary role of religion in human affairs. *Copies of any reports, proposals, or plans will be appreciated.*)

This questionnaire was sent to 47 chief state school officers; 213 superintendents of schools, nearly all in cities over 50,000; 158 presidents of state or municipal colleges or universities, not including the state teachers colleges; 547 presidents of church-related or independent colleges or universities; 171 presidents of state teachers colleges or state colleges which formerly were state teachers colleges; and 97 deans of schools of education or heads of departments of education in all types of institutions.

Usable responses were received as follows: chief state school officers, 24 (50 percent); superintendents of schools, nearly all in cities over 50,000, 82 (38 percent); presidents of state or municipal colleges or universities, 100 (64 percent); presidents of church-related or independent colleges or universities, 241 (44 percent); presidents of state teachers colleges, 80 (47 percent); deans of schools of education or heads of departments of education in all types of higher educational institutions, 29 (30 percent). Of the total of 1,233 questionnaires sent, 556, or 45 percent, were returned.

Those who cooperated by replying to the questionnaire were entirely self-selected. There was no direct follow-up. Discussion of the percentages of replies received from the several groups to the different instruments used in this inquiry is reserved for chapter iii, where we shall consider the opinions of educational and religious leaders on problems and issues involved in factual study of religion in the public schools.

We wish to make it entirely clear that the exploratory character of this study and the methods employed to obtain information require caution as to generalization. We have not attempted a comprehensive survey and, therefore, cannot answer many questions which may naturally arise as this report is read. We have indicated the sources of our information and confined our interpretation and conclusions to the data available.

Analysis of the replies and materials received reveals three patterns of practice which we have designated thus: *avoidance of religion, planned religious activities,* and *factual study of religion.* Admittedly, these are imperfect characterizations. There is much overlapping and often a single school system (even a single school), college, or university exhibits each of the three patterns; but usually one pattern is dominant. It is quite possible that respondents would classify their practices differently. A large quantity of materials, including many long letters, were received from which a few excerpts are reproduced below. While the practices as a whole tended to fall into a threefold classification, it was exceedingly difficult to select brief excerpts which illustrate one or another of the three categories. We, therefore, wish it to be entirely clear that the placing of particular illustrations is dependent on judgments of the staff and the committee, in the total context of the information available. The three patterns may be defined as follows:

1. *Avoidance of religion* is characterized by deliberate avoidance at one extreme and extends through accidental to merely incidental treatment at the other. Many assume that separation of church and state precludes anything more than general references to religion, and there is widespread fear that more specific references to religion in the school will incite public controversy and divide communities. A few believe that religion is irrelevant, inconsequential, or even detrimental to the aims of education. In large part, however, religion is avoided on prudential grounds.

2. *Planned religious activities* are characterized by definite, though often limited, provision for the treatment of religion

and for religious observances in the school. This category includes practices which have been objected to widely by certain religious groups and other practices which involve close cooperation with the church. These create disturbances in some communities.

Admittedly "planned religious activities" is a very general designation, but it appears adequate to embrace such varied activities as the following: devotional opening exercises, including the reading of the Bible, prayers, religious songs, and religious talks; religious programs in celebration of Thanksgiving, Hanukkah, Christmas, and Easter; grace before meals and prayers before athletic contests; sponsorship of religious clubs meeting in school buildings; the taking of Sunday school and church attendance census and encouragement of attendance at released time classes for religious instruction; elective courses in Bible; and credit toward high school graduation for Bible study outside of school. It is not our purpose here to approve or disapprove such practices, but rather to illustrate as accurately as possible the actual conditions revealed by the inquiry.

3. *Factual study of religion* is characterized by deliberate aim and definite plan to deal directly and factually with religion wherever and whenever it is intrinsic to learning experience in social studies, literature, art, music, and other fields. The aims of such study are to develop religious literacy, intelligent understanding of the role of religion in human affairs, and a sense of obligation to explore the resources that have been found in religion for achieving durable convictions and personal commitments. These aims arise from the requirements of general education which, to be effective, must view culture, human life, and personality whole.

Recognizing as we do the inherent limitations imposed upon the public school with respect to religion, we have deliberately chosen to focus our efforts on factual study of religion, which we believe any tax-supported school, college, or university can practice. This approach, we believe, offers the greatest promise of a solution to the problem.[2]

AVOIDANCE OF RELIGION

Contrary to the frequent assertion that there is and can be no religion in the public schools, we have found exceedingly few illustrations of deliberate avoidance in the replies to this inquiry. In view of the emphasis upon factual study of religion in the letters of transmittal and in the questionnaire, it is probable that many who think that such study is undesirable or inappropriate in the public schools did not reply. Considered from the point of view of what we think is desirable and feasible on educational grounds, avoidance of religion in some degree was found in all the replies and materials received. The illustrations reproduced below appear to us to fall short in greater or lesser degree of meeting a part of the responsibility of public education with respect to religion.

Practices in public elementary schools

The following illustrations were selected from all the replies and materials received from 12 chief state school officers and 57 superintendents of schools, principally in cities of over 50,000 population.

In our school system we carry on what are called Character Education programs once each month in each elementary and high school. [Superintendent, small city]

. . . . . .

We believe we are doing a quite adequate job in this area and have been for several years. Character building is undoubtedly one of the

[2] In our 1947 report we used the terms "objective teaching about religion" and "objective study of religion" interchangeably. In this study, throughout the conferences, questionnaires, and opinionnaires the first phrase was used. We now think "factual study of religion" is preferable because it emphasizes the activity of learners and more clearly differentiates this practice from "planned religious activities."

most important functions we have in the public schools and it is my opinion that we must strive to improve this process in every way possible. One of the best ways, perhaps, is to get the best teachers that can be obtained. [Superintendent, large city]

. . . . . .

We do teach the intangible spiritual values accidentally, incidentally —perhaps not as systematically as we should. [Superintendent, large city]

. . . . . .

In the elementary school there is little, if any, teaching about religion and religious institutions. Sometimes a casual remark or comment is made as an outgrowth of a story, an historical event, or a special holiday observance. . . . [Superintendent, county]

. . . . . .

We in this school district have felt rather strongly that the religious backgrounds of our children are part of the heritage in which all Americans share, and concerning which they should have some knowledge, but we have as yet failed to come up with any specific recommendations to teachers concerning valid approaches to this kind of school experience. [Superintendent, unified district]

. . . . . .

In the elementary curriculum there is no provision for dealing with religion or religious institutions, as such.

However, we do encourage participation in a Released Time Program. . . . For pupils who do not participate in this program and remain in school, a special curriculum developing moral and spiritual values is provided.

Attitudes of respect toward religion and toward religious beliefs of others are developed when situations arise which lend themselves to such a discussion. [Superintendent, small city]

Practices in public secondary schools

The following illustrations were selected from all the replies and materials received from 12 chief state school officers and 82 superintendents of schools, principally in cities of over 50,000 population.

It is my opinion that the public schools should not attempt to teach religion or about any religious institutions.   [Superintendent, small city]

. . . . . .

It is possible [to increase freedom of inquiry and discussion of religion], but we do not think it is needed.   The school is already doing what is necessary.   It is not our job to teach any one religion nor all religions.   Good schools are already teaching moral and spiritual values.   It is necessary that we maintain complete separation of church and state.   We must not permit meddling in the school administration by any church or church leader.   [Superintendent, small city]

. . . . . .

I have been a firm believer in separation of church and state.   However, I also realize that there are many instances in the classroom instruction whereby youngsters could be greatly encouraged and perhaps strengthened in their spiritual realizations if we were able to lean a bit further in that direction.   I would still be afraid to have any definite religious teaching in the schools.   . . .   I will have to continue to believe that it is better that we go on as we are today without any attempt to teach religious understandings in an objective manner.   [Superintendent, small city]

. . . . . .

At a recent staff and principals' meeting we discussed the problem [objective study of religion] in some detail and find that there is considerable disagreement in regard to the role which public education can play in this matter.   Several of the group are very much concerned over the traditional separation of church and state and feel that there is a great danger that the unity of the public school program could be torn asunder by an unfortunate handling of any matters pertaining to religion.   Without exception, the members of the council agreed that there is a great need for a better understanding of spiritual values and there can be no question but that an intelligent understanding of the role of religion in man's life is desirable.   [Superintendent, small city]

. . . . . .

Because of the peculiarly personal aspects of religion we make no attempt to bring about an organized program within the school curriculum.   Of course, days and events of special religious significance are given special attention through assembly programs, school newspapers, and classroom programs. But even in such cases as these, we find it necessary to avoid being offensive to certain religious concepts and backgrounds. [Superintendent, large city]

. . . . . .

We stress the major ideal of all true religion, namely the Brotherhood of Man. [Superintendent, large city]

Practices in state teachers colleges

We shall give particular attention to the state teachers colleges in illustrating what the colleges and universities are doing to prepare teachers for dealing with religion in the public schools for five reasons. First, the state teachers colleges are committed primarily to preparation of teachers for the public schools. Second, it is here that we should find, if anywhere, explicit and distinctive provisions, both in general education and in professional courses, for learning the theory and practice of relating religion to general education in the public schools. Third, these institutions are closer to the public school than other higher educational institutions and therefore should be sensitive to situations in local communities. Fourth, analysis of replies and materials received from presidents of all types of higher educational institutions reveals that the state teachers colleges as a group are fairly representative of practice in dealing with religion at the higher educational level. Fifth, relatively little attention has been given to what the teachers colleges are doing about religion.

It is generally recognized that the problem of dealing with religion at the higher educational level is different from that faced by the lower schools in two respects. Colleges and universities are relatively free in regard to factual study of religion; and since in most of these institutions a large proportion of students are away from their homes, colleges and universities are obligated to make provisions for programs of planned religious activities. Hence, the limitations indicated

by our normative hints for practice in the public schools cannot apply with equal force to higher educational institutions.

The illustrations presented below were selected from replies of 80 presidents of state teachers colleges, or of members
of their staffs.

There is nothing in our curricular activities that I know about.
Extraclass activities deal with specifics, not with religion or religious
institutions which would promote understanding of the role of religion
in human affairs.   [President]

. . . . . .

We have no specific curricula dealing with religion and religious institutions.   We do have several extraclass organizations, both inter-
denominational and denominational . . . which are carried on
by the respective churches on this campus. [President]

. . . . . .

Our curriculum does not in any way directly concern itself with the
role of religion in human affairs.   There are indirect references to
religion in many courses, since it forms a part of the culture.

We might do two things a little better on our campus.   We might
offer courses dealing directly with the historical and contemporary
role of religion in human affairs and we might construct units in our
general education program which would cover this area.   [President]

PLANNED RELIGIOUS ACTIVITIES

In contrast to the extremely limited number of illustrations of deliberate avoidance of religion found in replies and
material received, nearly all public elementary and secondary
schools and state teachers colleges exhibit some examples of
planned religious activities.   Considered wholly within the
limitations of the information received, the dominant pattern
of practice in public education would appear to be a variety
of planned religious activities; but, as noted above, we think
avoidance of religion is more representative of current practice.   The illustrations reproduced below seem to us, in
greater or lesser degree, to exemplify the "planned religious
activities" approach to this problem.

Practices in the public elementary schools

One pre-school faculty workshop here this year was devoted to improving the moral and spiritual educational program in our schools. We have always felt that one of the fundamentals of education in this Christian democracy is the strengthening of the basic teachings of religion. [Superintendent, large city]

. . . . . .

—— has a State Board of Character Education and Accredited Bible Study. . . . The committee prepares materials which may be used in the regular classroom situations as well as in extraclass activities carried on under state laws with regard to released time. [Chief state school officer]

. . . . . .

The curricula and extraclass activities are based upon the principles of a basic religion. Respect for God, for religion, for the home, for fellowmen, for law, and a love of these are taught. . . . While we believe in the separation of church and state, we feel that it is impossible to avoid the teaching of the place of religion in human activities and great movements. [Chief state school officer]

. . . . . .

An informal survey of what is being done in the elementary schools of —— to provide a spiritual message in the daily program reveals the following emphases: singing religious songs; appreciating religious books, poems, stories (including Bible stories); saying grace and prayers; listening to selected readings from the Bible; and taking part in character building activities. [Superintendent, large city]

. . . . . .

—— was the first city in the state to undertake the teaching of the Bible in the schools. . . . In the elementary schools the teachers visit the schools once a week and have the children in grades four, five, and six for thirty minutes. Any child whose parents wish is excused. Very few ask for this privilege. . . . [Superintendent, large city]

. . . . . .

In our elementary schools most of the rooms offer thanks before eating their lunches. A prayer song is used in some of the rooms while

others have different children of different faiths offer thanks. [Super-
intendent, large city]

. . . . . .

In practically all our elementary classrooms in the public schools,
daily devotionals conducted by the students are carried on. Students
read the scriptures, sing hymns, offer prayers, and occasionally someone comes in to talk for ten minutes at a general assembly. [Super-
intendent, large city]

. . . . . .

At all times we exercise care that any religious emphasis shall be
nonsectarian. We have emphasized values that underlie many great
religions. . . . Faith in and reverence for God—a power greater
than oneself—we have included as basic in our Judaeo-Christian
heritage. Opportunities for experiencing faith and reverence grow
naturally from subjects such as art, music, and literature. Science
offers opportunities for experiencing a sense of reverence for the
wonders of the universe—the vastness of time and space. Prayers of
a general, nonsectarian nature, the use of the Bible as literature,
meditation, and discussion of inspirational quotations, inspirational
nonsectarian programs, voluntary worship groups—all of these
activities, carried on at appropriate times and places, emphasize
religion as a part of the culture, and as an important factor in the
lives of individuals. Religion is regarded as one of the great humanities, and loyalty to the church of one's choice is encouraged. [Super-
intendent, large city]

The following resolution was passed by the New York
State Board of Regents, November 30, 1951. We quote it
in full because we think it illustrates the concern of many people that some method be found to give appropriate recognition to religion in the corporate life of the public school.

Belief in and dependence upon Almighty God was the very corner-
stone upon which our Founding Fathers builded. Our State Constitution opens with these solemn words: "We, the People of the State
of New York, grateful to Almighty God for our Freedom, in order
to secure these blessings, do establish this Constitution."

We are convinced that this fundamental belief and dependence of
the American—always a religious—people is the best security against
the dangers of these difficult days. In our opinion, the securing of

the peace and safety of our country and our State against such dangers points to the essentiality of teaching our children, as set forth in the Declaration of Independence, that Almighty God is their Creator, and that by Him they have been endowed with their inalienable rights of life, liberty, and the pursuit of happiness.

We believe that at the commencement of each school day the act of allegiance to the Flag might well be joined with this act of reverence to God: "Almighty God, we acknowledge our dependence upon Thee, and we beg Thy blessings upon us, our parents, our teachers and our Country."

We believe that the school day thus started might well include specific programs stressing the moral and spiritual heritage which is America's, the trust which our pioneering ancestors placed in Almighty God, their gratitude to Him from Whom they freely and frequently acknowledged came their blessings and their freedom and their abiding belief in the free way of life and in the universal brotherhood of man based upon their acknowledgment of the fatherhood of their Creator, Almighty God, Whom they loved and reverenced in diverse ways.

We believe that thus constantly confronted with the basic truth of their existence and inspired by the example of their ancestors, our children will find all their studies brought into focus and accord; respect for lawful authority and obedience to law will be the natural concomitant of their growth, and each of them will be properly prepared to follow the faith of his or her father, as he or she receives the same at mother's knee, by father's side, and as such faith is expounded and strengthened for them by his or her religious leaders.

We believe that thus the school will fulfill its high function of supplementing the training of the home, ever intensifying in the child that love for God, for parents and for home which is the mark of true character training and the sure guarantee of a country's welfare.

We believe that such is the best way of insuring that this Government and our way of life shall not perish from the earth.

We believe that this Statement will be subscribed to by all men and women of good will, and we call upon all of them to aid in giving life to our program.

Practices in the public secondary schools

We seek only to teach the existence of a Supreme Being and to develop an attitude of reverence toward a Supreme Being. We do not provide for the discussion of the historical and contemporary role of religion in human affairs. We do cooperate fully with our local churches and seek to encourage church attendance. [Superintendent, large city]

.   .   .   .   .   .

All schools . . . have a morning devotion each day at which time a Bible story or passage is read without comment and a prayer is offered. This prayer may be the Lord's Prayer or other formal or informal prayer. In the secondary schools the devotion is planned and presented by student groups using the inter-classroom communication system. These groups, including Y-Teens, Hi-Y, Student Council, and speech classes, are, of course, assisted and supervised by their teachers or sponsors.

The Y-Teens and Hi-Y, which have been mentioned, are both sponsored within the school activity program and function as extracurricular activities. . . . [Superintendent, small city]

.   .   .   .   .   .

In the Bible teaching that is being done on school time [in school buildings], a very earnest attempt is made to keep free from all creeds and dogmas and a sincere effort is made to recognize good in other religions and in all creeds. We actually have Jews, Protestants, and Catholics learning together and helping to pay for the program. Various churches in the city and interested individuals contribute to the support of the teachers. The funds are pooled and are sent to our office which is responsible for the payment of salaries of the teachers. Although there is an active advisory committee, the teachers are employed by the Board of Education and are subject to the regulations of all teachers. [Teachers have homeroom assignments and are considered regular members of high school faculties. Courses are elective.] [Superintendent, large city]

Following is a brief description of a devotional program in a senior high school. It was chosen from a number of such illustrations.

Essentially, the impetus for the series [of devotional programs] came from a panel discussion presented by members of an English class on the question: "What steps can be taken to reconcile religious differences in a democracy?" The conclusions stimulated further inquiry into the responsibility of the school in combating religious illiteracy.

In due time, the Student Council, deploring the prevalent scanty thought given to morning exercises, organized for action. After several searching discussions by the Council, a committee of six students, representing as many denominations, was appointed to investigate the possibilities of a devotional series as one way of meeting an expressed need.

The following procedure was subsequently outlined: An eight-to-ten minute broadcast [over the public address system of the school] consisting of four parts—a musical prelude, a secular reading, a correlative passage from the Bible, and the Lord's Prayer. The purposes of the series were then specified as follows:

1. To promote Christianity as an ethical way of life.
2. To emphasize the basic truths that all creeds have in common.
3. To strengthen religious foundations.
4. To foster an appreciation of the Bible as living literature.
5. To present a realistic approach to the solution of ethical problems that confront young people.
6. To consider the contributions to religious thought of philosophers, poets, novelists, and essayists.

Additional aims not set down but carefully noted were:

1. To recognize fully the function of the church and home in doctrinal instruction.
2. To avoid evangelical fervor and pietistic preachment.
3. To attend meticulously to the mechanical aspects of the broadcasts, to preparation of scripts, and the rehearsing of student participants.

The first broadcasts, presented during Holy Week, consisted of recorded music from Handel's *Messiah;* selections from the poetry of Edwin Arlington Robinson and Frederick C. Boden; Biblical passages concerning the Last Supper, Christ's visit to Gethsemane, the trial before Pilate, and the Crucifixion; and the Lord's Prayer (the student reader began the Lord's Prayer and was faded out as the students in their homerooms repeated the prayer in unison). [Principal, senior high school, small city]

The following extracts are quoted from a published report of a Council of Christian Education in a community. Such instruction was reported as quite general in some states.

The ——— Council of Christian Education was organized in 1946 by the churches of ——— to assist parents and Sunday Schools in the growing demand for a more adequate Christian Education of our youth.

A program of Christian Education was begun in the autumn of 1946 by which Biblical Literature was taught in the high school. The program, approved and adopted by the School Board, brought into its classes 90 percent of the high school enrollment.

The work of teaching was done by two local ministers on behalf of the Protestants and by the local priest for the Roman Catholics. The success of the project was such that the Council, representing the Protestant churches, at the close of the third semester employed a full-time teacher to continue the work. The Reverend ———, a qualified public school teacher and minister, began his work of teaching in January, 1948.

[After the Supreme Court decision in the McCollum case in 1948]. . . . Consultation was immediately held with the school authorities and with the State Department of Education. A plan was worked out by the Council and approved by the School Board whereby courses in Sacred Literature were continued in the high school. This plan works within the bounds of the Supreme Court decision and under the laws of ———.

The courses in Sacred Literature are now an integral part of the high school curriculum. They are correlated with the courses in History and English. Reverend —— is a member of the high school faculty. His salary is underwritten by the Council.

Enrollment in these courses is up to the pupils and to the interest of parents. In 1948, 51 percent of the high school enrollment were enrolled in courses in Sacred Literature. For the school year beginning in 1949, 42.9 percent enrollment had been attained. . . . For the academic year 1950–51 the voluntary enrollment reached 53 percent. . . . [The courses offered are described as follows:]

Grade nine

Religious biography—this course is introduced with specific reference to the book *One God* by Florence Mary Fitch. The aim is appreciation and understanding of the Jewish, Roman Catholic, and Protestant ways of worship. Emphasis is given to "a nation under God." Old Testament personalities are studied; so also the life and work of St. Paul. Each student makes a study of the life of his own Church founder.

Grade ten

Comparative Religion—a survey course of the major religions of the world. Emphasis is given to the influence of religion upon the culture of a nation. The course parallels the tenth grade studies of the History of Civilization. The textbook used is *This Believing World* by Lewis Browne, together with *The Bible of the World.* The Gospel record is the source of material for the study of the life of Christ.

Grade eleven

The Bible as Living Literature—students are acquainted with the content of the Bible in its literary forms. The course is developed on the groundwork of related courses in English. Every effort is made to present an appreciation of the spiritual values of the Holy Scriptures which underlie its great literature. Evaluation is made of content of the English Bible as literature.

Grade twelve

Ethics for Our Day—in a day of uncertainty about conflicting ways of life and the problems of youth in choosing right and wrong, this course is most effective. It attempts to inspire an appreciation of Christian principles in a democratic way of life. Self-analysis is supplemented with a study of behavior patterns in relation to the family, the school, and study is made of those forces in the modern world which threaten to destroy our Christian and democratic heritage. [Council of Christian Education, small city]

Practices in state teachers colleges

Our college works with the churches of our community in different ways. Each church is provided with a list of students belonging to the particular denomination. During the freshman week of orientation one night is set aside for all freshmen and transfer students to go to a designated place on the campus to meet the pastors and workers of that church of which they are members, or have expressed a preference for. The churches have scheduled nights for the students to have parties at the churches. All of the churches have these parties on the same night. . . . The college has for many years had a YWCA and YMCA. [President]

. . . . . .

We are giving a good deal of thought on the ——— College campus to the subject of religion in higher education. . . . we added a man to our faculty this fall in the fields of religion and philosophy. . . .

Our new college auditorium is fully equipped for Christian worship. Vesper services are held at various times through the school year, and noontime services are held during Holy Week. In these services we use hymnals and a complete altar set donated by a friend of the College. [President]   . . . . . .

On every Tuesday evening throughout the college year no activities except religious activities take place on this campus. We have student leaders conduct devotional services at all College assemblies. This practice has commanded great respect and reverence from the entire student body. We have an Inter-Religious Council consisting of student leaders of Protestant, Catholic, and Jewish groups, together with their spiritual advisers, who meet regularly and undertake projects which can be pursued without embarrassment to anyone. . . . Each year the Inter-Religious Council sponsors Religion in Life Week, the World Student Service Fund, and lately they have adopted an orphan child in a war-torn country. . . .

The foregoing patterns of practice have produced an attitude of tolerance, reverence, and a consciousness of the moral and spiritual side which a teacher should reflect. In view of the fact that we are a teacher education institution providing teachers for the public schools, we are keenly interested in the closest approximation possible of such goals. [President]
. . . . . .

This state institution is attempting to be a Christian college in reality, as well as in name. As a teacher preparatory institution we feel our responsibility keenly. I am sure that in this whole matter of religion and spiritual values, the knowledge, philosophy, and character of the teacher is the most important factor.

We find that a large number of our students are so confused as to their own religious beliefs that they really don't know what to do. To meet this lack, the College is offering an elective course called Christian Doctrine. This course . . . is taught by pastors in the city. At present a Lutheran pastor is offering this course for Lutheran students, and a Catholic priest is giving it for Catholic students. . . . We have another two-hour course called Christian Ethics. This is also taught by the pastors in the city. [President]
. . . . . .

We have a Department of Religious Education. This department offers a major. . . . This college also sponsors Noon-Day Devotionals conducted by students under the direction of ———, Professor of Religious Education. From time to time assembly programs of a religious nature are conducted. In the spring of each year we sponsor what the College calls Religious Emphasis Week. Our problem is to secure a larger participation on the part of students in our various programs of religious education. This is our chief concern. [President]

. . . . . .

The curriculum in Religious Education includes the following specific courses: Old Testament Survey, New Testament Survey, Era of Renaissance and Reformation, The Teachings of Jesus, The Teachings of the Hebrew Prophets, World Religions, Ethics, Introduction to Philosophy, and Work Experience in Religious Education.

In addition to the above, a ——— Bible Chair has been established near the college campus. [President]

FACTUAL STUDY OF RELIGION

The following illustrations of factual study of religion meet only *partially* the requirements of the definition given above. While a few illustrations of this approach to the problem were found even in the public elementary schools, such illustrations were found much less frequently at all levels of public education than were illustrations of planned religious activities. It seems probable that illustrations of factual study were reported in larger proportion to actual practice than were planned religious activities or avoidance of religion, particularly the latter. The character of this inquiry as indicated by the definition on the letterhead[3] of the project and by the questions emphasized factual study of religion.

Practices in public elementary schools

The curricular and extracurricular activities of the public schools in this regard are determined by the local school officials. The following are some of the activities of certain local school systems in this area:
. . . (*b*) reading selections from great writers dealing with religion; (*c*) social studies classes have a unit on World Religions as a part

[3] See p. 93.

of their course in World History. Religious holidays and events are observed in many schools. [Chief state school officer]

. . . . . .

In connection with the study of community life, children occasionally visit Jewish, Catholic, and Protestant centers of worship where talks on special customs are given by clergymen or their representatives. Religious beliefs of peoples of the world are mentioned, especially in the intermediate grades, where pupils are studying about different countries and civilizations. The film *One God* was shown in one school to all sixth grades who desired to see it. Sometimes matters pertaining to religion come up during discussions of science. . . . [Superintendent, small city]

. . . . . .

In one sixth grade social studies program a definite part of the time is spent in discussion of the growth of the church and various religions and the contributions that they have made to our present civilization. The history of the Hebrew nation as a race of the ancient world is studied. Our courses in American history in grades five, seven, eight, and eleven all provide opportunity for an intelligent discussion of the place of religion in the life of the American people. World history in grades nine and ten expands the study that was made at the sixth grade level. [Superintendent, large city]

. . . . . .

We would find it neither possible nor desirable to study any culture in our social studies program without some attention to the religion and the religious customs of the culture. As a few brief examples: a unit on Early California History naturally gives attention to the California missions; a unit on Mexico brings us into consideration of such matters as the Christmas Procession and other religious festivals; a unit on Man and His Records deals, of course, with such things as Egyptian, Babylonian, and Phoenician customs and emphasizes the important part which religion played in those cultures and in the development of written records. [Superintendent, large city]

. . . . . .

At several points in the curriculum attention is specifically drawn to the religious life of the community. Chapters in the Story of ———, locally written, at the fourth-grade level and another at the ninth grade, present some data concerning ——— churches. Several teachers . . . carry on projects each year which involve class trips to various neighborhood churches and some study of the faiths represented. In many cases some effort is made to understand the Jewish Hanukkah festival at the same time Christmas is being celebrated. [Superintendent, large city]

. . . . . .

Our social studies program in the elementary school is a study of the ever-widening community of the pupil. It starts with the home, moves into the school, and community, then into the state, etc. The institutions which bear directly upon the culture of the people in these communities are dealt with, and the contributions which they make to the culture are treated extensively. No attempt is made to determine the specific creed of a particular church, no attempt is made to study the organization within the various churches, and no comparisons are made between the different churches. They, the pupils, do become increasingly aware, however, of the function of the church in the community. [Director of teaching, state teachers college, campus laboratory school]

. . . . . .

. . . as groups of teachers and administrators have worked in both the elementary and secondary areas of curriculum, there has evolved the concept that intercultural understanding and appreciation of the religious-cultural heritage of our people should serve as a "strand of experience" to be woven throughout the instructional program. At certain levels and in certain areas of the program where it seems appropriate in terms of needs of young people, special emphasis should be given to this continuous strand of experience . . . particularly in grades fifth and sixth is there wide opportunity to examine religious and spiritual values in their cultural setting. [Superintendent, large city]

Practices in the public secondary schools

There is no formal course in the understanding of the role of religion. . . . We do, however, stress informal instruction of this nature as questions arise in our courses. [Superintendent, large city]

. . . . . .

. . . we have a committee which is making an analysis of the moral and spiritual values in our present program. For example, our junior high English teachers have prepared a brief summary of the material used in the field of literature and the moral and religious implications of each selection. . . . It makes an interesting showing when it is pulled together in summary form and it surprised our people who have been teaching the materials. [Superintendent, small city]

. . . . .

In certain history classes every student reports on his religious background. In a certain senior class which is based on the Great Books technique the Book of Job is studied as literature, but growing out of the discussions, deep religious problems come to life. [Superintendent, township]

. . . . .

The senior sociology classes have as an annual practice invited representatives of various faiths to interpret their beliefs and to answer questions. [Superintendent, township]

. . . . .

Two years ago, the ———— Public Schools developed a course of study for the ninth grade . . . which is entitled Living in ————. In this course . . . we cover such topics as: History of the Community; Home Life in ————; Your Government; . . . and Places of Worship in ————. . . . We speak of the development of the churches in ———— and we emphasize the fact that Jews, Catholics, and Protestants live side by side and accept the Old Testament of the same Bible with variations of different parts. We teach that all three believe in one God. We make a spot map on which a child places the churches of the community. . . . [Superintendent, small city]

. . . . .

In our secondary schools, religious institutions as a part of the culture are studied in both eighth- and eleventh-grade American History and in tenth-grade World History. At the present time we are planning a new tenth-grade citizenship course which will include a unit entitled Man's Search for Religion. . . . We also have elective courses in which the Bible is studied as great literature. [Superintendent, large city]

. . . . .

In ———— County we have felt free to teach about religions for at least five years. Such a unit is now in progress in a ninth-grade core class. . . . The faiths represented in the community are studied, explained, reported upon by children of the church and discussed. The work includes visits to Catholic, Protestant, and Jewish places of worship. . . . The aim is an intelligent understanding that will let the child sincerely respect the practices and beliefs of his neighbors and to show that the true practice of these faiths is uplifting. . . . [Supervisor, county]

. . . . . .

In our junior high schools, we have been developing the core curriculum program under the title Unified Studies, for several years. The Unified Studies course, which occupies two hours daily, is now required of all junior high school pupils in the seventh and eighth grades. These classes follow the core method of studying whole problems as related to life, cutting across department barriers. In some of these . . . groups, the pupils and teachers have undertaken to deal with religion and religious institutions as a part of the culture in a very successful way. Some of these groups have spent several weeks on this topic, making field trips to the many churches in the city, and using as resource persons several of the Jewish rabbis, Catholic priests, and Protestant ministers who are willing to assist. From our experience with the study of religion through the core curriculum, my belief is this offers by far the most promising approach to the study of religion as a part of the culture in the public schools. We have had no adverse community reactions to the projects undertaken. . . . [Superintendent, large city]

The following is an extract from a report of a superintendent whose staff went to considerable pains to study practices in their school system before replying to the questionnaire:

Religion as an area of study in the curriculum is covered mainly in the teaching of the social studies. This topic is treated in two ways: (1) as an integral part of the sequence of chronological events which record the history of man's progress; (2) as a special area for consideration in a unit in World History which outlines a study of art, music, religion, etc., in a setting of cultural development.

Religion as an experience of mankind is taught in the World History course where the great religions are considered in their historical settings. This study includes the teaching, influence, and contributions of each of the religions. In order that the purposes of the teaching may be understood and effectively attained, there has been general agreement on each of the following points or concepts:

1. Religion has been a universal experience of mankind.
2. Religion has been a great cultural force in man's history.
3. Religion has made great contributions to our ethical heritage.
4. Those aspects of the various religious groups which are common to all should be emphasized, rather than the differences which are divisive.
5. We should recognize the right of all men to choose the forms of their religious expression.
6. We should understand and respect the religions and religious practices which differ from our own.

The program in English includes the study or casual reading of many literary works expressing religious feelings.

The art teacher reports: "In my art classes, religion has been brought in through the designing of Christmas cards, wrapping paper, and other projects. In addition, I have had each class work on its own mural showing how Christmas is celebrated in a different country. . . . A great deal can be taught . . . about Renaissance religious art and Oriental culture in art appreciation classes."

We encourage the festival spirit of the December season through use of the music of all the major faiths . . , and through . . . participation in the appropriate vocal and instrumental music as adapted to the seasons of Hanukkah and Christmas. We have advanced understanding by class work, assembly sings, and public concerts where the stories and music of Hanukkah and Christmas have been presented by a combination of all faiths. . . . Sometimes leaders of these faiths have been invited to be present at these events so that they might, in their own words, tell the backgrounds and religious implications of such seasonal religious events. . . . With the cooperation of the ———— Music Society, the choral groups of the high school have annually presented a community rendition of Handel's great oratorio, *The Messiah,* in which adults and students of all faiths participate. [Superintendent, small city]

Following is an illustration of the way one high school attempts to deal with religion in a coordinated program of instruction in art, history, literature, and music and in an experimental seminar on religions for seniors.

As a part of the World Culture course given in the tenth, eleventh, and twelfth grades, the tenth-grade social studies course covers man from his earliest beginnings down to about 1800 A.D. and the literature course surveys the religious literature, including the Bible as an anthology of Hebrew and Early Christian literature, Greek literature, and the Koran, some of the sacred literatures of the Orient and the religious classics of early Europe, the Middle Ages, the Renaissance and Puritan literature. In the social studies course one full unit of five weeks is devoted to religion. Religion as an influencing factor is included in other units.

The teachers of English, history, art, and music correlate their teaching. The music teacher acquaints the pupils with the various types of music developed by these religious groups. The art teacher directs the examination of other forms of art evolved by religious groups. The English teacher plans the readings of the class so that they may read and try to interpret the underlying philosophies of these religions. The history teacher establishes the historical setting and tries to pull the materials together through discussion sessions. Fundamentally the [coordinated teaching] strives to bring about the following understandings:

1. Why man, at any point in his development, has a need for religion.
2. How man has used religion.
3. The geographic and historic environment in which different religions have developed.
4. The similarity and differences between major religions of the world. (This is aimed at bringing about more tolerant attitudes through better understandings.)
5. The influence of religion upon history.

The religions studied are: Taoism, Brahmanism, Buddhism, Confucianism, Shintoism, Judaism, Mohammedanism, and Christianity. Aside from the classroom approach, trips are planned to museums, a synagogue, and a Roman Catholic Church, and panel discussions are arranged by Protestant clergy.

[In the twelfth grade a Seminar on Religions was introduced this year as an experiment. The instructor is a member of the faculty of the college in the community, and his salary is paid by contributions of the churches.] The purpose of this course is to outline the main beliefs held by the world's religions. However, as much time is given to a study of the beliefs and problems of Judaism and

Christianity as to the rest of the religions combined. This is due to
our recognition that these are the faiths which have molded our particular society and are therefore of primary interest to us.

In addition to outlining the beliefs of religions, we are attempting
to stimulate the student to think through his own religious convictions. For this purpose several of the problems that face the religions are raised. For example, we will raise such questions as: "Is
there a God?"; "What is the relation of religion to ethics?"; "How
is God known and approached?"; "What is the Christian Way of
life?" In answering these and similar questions, the student will be
introduced to the varying answers given in our culture. . . . [Prin-
cipal, senior high school, small city]

Practices in the state teachers colleges

It seems to me that all teachers in training should have a general
knowledge of existing religions and know their basic philosophies.
This might be done in history of religions. So far it has been elective. I am wondering if it would be accepted as a requirement in
all public teacher education institutions. [President]

. . . . . .

In the ——— Teachers College a program of general education
was instituted in 1945 which included, under the heading of Personal
Development, a course in either the World's Great Religions or in an
Introduction to Philosophy. The choice is left to the student.
Some, whose religious training has been well provided for, choose
the philosophy course. A few others shy away from the course in
religion. Many, however, welcome this course and the opportunity
to learn about religion in the life of man. The course is taught
by the President of the College. In this college, located in a pre-
dominantly Christian community and region, our teachers receive
a considerable amount of religious instruction, on a broad basis,
through literature and history courses and through the laboratory-
school student-teaching experience, since much of the work of literature, art, music, and elementary social studies immediately preceding Christmas and Easter brings out the origin and celebrations of
these festivals in our own and other countries. [Dean]

. . . . . .

[One teachers college reports a projected course in the Department of Education on the Teaching of Moral and Spiritual Values
in Public Schools, the outline of which contains units on:]

The Nature of the Spiritual and Moral Problems Challenging
   Teachers in the Public Schools
The Meaning, Nature, and Source of Moral and Spiritual Values
Moral and Social Freedom
Religion in the Public School
Moral and Spiritual Values and School Practice
                                        [Professor of education]

. . . . . .

I have been experimenting for several years now with the teaching *about* religion in our senior seminar in sociology. . . . It is
our practice now to invite in a pastor representing the Catholics,
one representing the Protestants, and a Jewish rabbi. We invite
these pastors to give an hour's lecture and discussion on the history,
theology, and organization of their particular faith. [Professor of
sociology]

. . . . . .

As a state college, ———— Teachers College confines its curricular
emphasis upon religion and religious institutions to two integrated
courses—one in social studies and one in humanities—and to two
courses in the Bible, the Old Testament and the New Testament. . . .
   Perhaps an elective pedagogical course in the Education Department might be offered to future teachers if the course were taught
objectively and discreetly. As a teacher of the two courses in the
Bible, I have found, especially during summer sessions, that teachers
are very much interested in them. [Professor of English]

. . . . . .

Two years ago the State Board of Education approved a Department of Philosophy and Religion. . . . This department contains
the usual courses on the History of Religion, Philosophy of Religion,
etc. [President]

. . . . . .

In classes in Elementary Education there is discussion of the relationship of religion and religious tolerance to the child's developing
personality. . . . Religious institutions are . . . studied in our
courses in sociology and indirectly in courses in literature where
religious literature is often specially treated. The course in Social

Psychology gives some attention to the origins and the development of religious behavior. Some of the courses in rural education deal with the rural church as a community institution. . . . The origin and historical development and contemporary role of religions is quite adequately treated in our course in Western Civilization. . . . A required course for all English majors includes religions and religious philosophies. [Assistant to the president]

. . . . . .

We offer eight courses in religion which are open to students on a strictly elective basis. In addition, we have included one course which will meet a specific requirement in our new curriculum. . . . This course is called The Heritage of the Bible and a student must complete this course or one entitled Introduction to Philosophy. Some attention is also given to religious institutions in courses in sociology and to the development of religious ideas in the humanities courses required of all students. [Following are the titles of courses in religion:]

The Bible as Literature
The Heritage of the Bible
Christian Ethics
Religions of the World
History of Christianity
Introduction to Religious Ideas
Problems of Religion
Teaching Religion
Introduction to Philosophy
                        [President]

Practices in Other Colleges and Universities Compared with the Practices of Teachers Colleges

To do justice to the practices of church-related, independent, and the public colleges and universities, other than the state teachers colleges, as revealed by replies and materials received, would require a very extensive section in this report, or a separate report. Since this inquiry is concerned principally with the public elementary and secondary schools and teacher education, we shall present merely a tabulation indicating relative emphasis on methods of dealing with religion in these institutions in comparison with the methods employed in the teachers colleges, and a brief summary of generalizations based upon our analysis of all the materials received from presidents or members of their staffs. The practices of the state teachers colleges are believed to be fairly typical of the patterns exhibited by other higher educational institutions, except for relative emphasis.

Table 1 in the Appendix (see page 95) presents a tabulation of replies to the first question of the first questionnaire, indicating rank orders of frequency of mention of the methods employed by the colleges and universities in dealing with religion, as revealed by this inquiry. It should be emphasized that the replies to the questionnaire were free. Each president reported what he thought to be relevant and important. The staff of the inquiry determined the categories under which the various methods mentioned were tabulated. Thus, a rough measure was attained of what is actually being done and of the relative importance of the various methods, as viewed by the respondents.

The following generalizations about the practices of the church-related, independent, and tax-supported colleges and universities in comparison with the state teachers colleges appear to be warranted:

1. *Characteristics of the practice of church-related colleges and universities.*—Broadly speaking, all church-related colleges and universities, as differentiated from independent and publicly controlled institutions of higher learning, present a distinctive general pattern of practice in dealing with religion. The principal characteristics of this pattern may be summarized under two heads: the place given religion in the total corporate life of these institutions, and the particular methods employed to maintain this place for religion.

Religion is viewed, in greater or lesser degree, as a basic human need, an integrating motive for human activity, and the source of ultimate values. It is therefore assumed to be integral with the ends and the means of education. This conception is reflected in such statements as these: "Our conception of religion as fundamental truth (plus the application of this truth to living) permeates the thinking of our professors. This thinking, being basic in nature and organic in its development, helps to clarify and interpret subject matter in other fields. Students imbibe this fundamental thinking in every course they take. We find religion the most powerful integrating force in education"; "In a church-related college such as ours, I believe we must aim at nothing less than a Christian integration of all knowledge"; and "The faculty has accepted as their philosophy of education and as their objective the development of individuals well-rounded with respect to body, mind, and spirit, and having a thirst for knowledge, a desire to serve their fellowmen, and an abiding faith in God."

As a group, these colleges and universities exhibit the pattern of *planned religious activities*. Explicit or implicit throughout the materials received is the aim to make students religious through instruction, example, and practice.

The methods employed by the church-related institutions to attain these ends are differentiated from the methods employed by the state teachers colleges, for whatever ends, in several respects. They place greater reliance than do the teachers colleges on required courses in religion, maintenance of a department of religion, dealing with religion when and where intrinsic to other courses, and required attendance at chapel or other religious assemblies. On the other hand, the church-related institutions place less reliance than do the teachers colleges on religious foundations on or near the campus, encouragement and facilitation of student denominational groups, and voluntary attendance at chapel or other religious assemblies.

2. *Characteristics of the practice of independent colleges and universities.*—There is much greater variation in practice among the independent colleges and universities than among the church-related institutions. At one extreme their practices are indistinguishable from those of some of the church-related institutions, and at the other extreme they are indistinguishable from those of the tax-supported colleges and universities. As a group, however, they do exhibit an almost unanimous avowal of the importance of religion in general education and a recognition of institutional responsibility for meeting the religious needs of students. A second characteristic is greater freedom of choice of methods on the part of students than is true of the church-related institutions. They tend, therefore, in varying degree to exhibit within given institutions both the pattern of *planned religious activities* and *factual study of religion,* more often than is true of the church-related colleges and universities.

In comparison with the state teachers colleges, the independent institutions place greater reliance on maintenance of a department of religion, courses in religion in other departments, required courses in religion, dealing with religion when intrinsic to other courses, employment of a chaplain or religious counselor, required attendance at chapel or other religious assemblies, elective courses in religion, and units on religion in required core courses. The independent institutions place less reliance than do the teachers colleges on Religious Emphasis Week, religious foundations on or near the campus, encouragement and facilitation of denominational groups, voluntary attendance at chapel or other religious assemblies, interfaith councils, and cooperation with local churches.

3. *Characteristics of the practice of the tax-supported colleges and universities other than state teachers colleges.*—The practices of these institutions are very similar to those of state

teachers colleges, as indicated in Table 1 (page 95). The only marked differences are more frequent maintenance of a department of religion, the offering of courses in religion in other departments, and fewer units on religion in required core courses than is true of the state teachers colleges.

SUMMARY

The answer to the question, "How are the public elementary and secondary schools dealing with religion?" is threefold. A few school systems appear to avoid religion deliberately, but they are a very small minority of those participating in this inquiry. However, avoidance of a part of the responsibility of the public schools inadvertently through neglect or failure to deal with the facts and implications of religion intrinsic to the curriculum, was found in greater or lesser degree in all the replies and materials received. Nearly all the school systems participating in this study make some provision for planned religious activities. This pattern varies in both character and extent, but it appears to be almost universal. It should be pointed out, however, that such activities as we have classified as falling within this category may, and perhaps often do, give a false impression that the schools are doing all that needs to be done about religion. A considerable number of public school systems are experimenting with factual study of religion in one or more areas, particularly in the social studies program. Often a single school system, and even a single school, exhibits all three patterns of practice.

The answer to the second question, "How are the colleges and universities preparing teachers to deal with religion in the public schools?" is less complete. So far as the general education of prospective teachers is concerned, it is probable that they receive little, if any, special consideration. Analysis of the materials received reveals the same threefold patterns of practice found in the elementary and secondary schools.

It is significant, we think, that only a few of the presidents of church-related colleges and universities, the state teachers colleges, and other tax-supported higher educational institutions made special mention of the responsibility of their institutions for the preparation of teachers to deal with this problem in the public schools. The tax-supported teacher education institutions of one state have been cooperating with the state department of education during the past four summers in workshops designed to assist teachers in developing moral and spiritual values in the public schools. Other such workshops have been conducted and are being projected. But as far as our data reveal the facts, only one state university has proposed a course or a workshop to deal explicitly with the problems, methods, and techniques of factual study of religion in the public schools. Even in this instance the proposed title of the course or workshop is "Moral and Spiritual Values in Public Education." While the questionnaire did not raise this question explicitly, it was implicit in the total context of the inquiry as presented in the letter of transmittal and the first questionnaire. Further consideration will be given to the answer to this question in chapter iv.

The third question raised at the beginning of this chapter was, "How do these practices conform to the alternative of factual study of religion and the frame of reference for this inquiry stated in chapter i?" We have found a few illustrations of this practice at all levels of public education. Comments of many educational administrators seem to us to warrant the assumption that the position we have taken will be supported when it is more fully understood. As will be seen in chapter iii, educational and religious leaders tend to think that factual study of religion in the public schools is desirable.

The illustrations of practice at all levels of public education strikingly reveal the fact that there is no clear-cut and generally observed policy with respect to the relation of religion to public education. The concern expressed by educational administrators in their comments regarding this inquiry—whether favorable, doubtful, or unfavorable—all indicate that *the function of the public schools in dealing with religion is no longer an academic question.*

CHAPTER III

OPINIONS OF EDUCATIONAL AND RELIGIOUS LEADERS

ARE educational and religious leaders prepared to undertake cooperative studies and experiments to determine the place that should be given to religion in public education? How are our proposed factual study of religion and the conclusions stated in chapter i appraised by those who have cooperated in the inquiry?

Data needed for answering these questions were obtained from three sources: conferences with educational and religious leaders, responses of educational leaders to questionnaires, and responses of educational and religious leaders to opinionnaires. These methods of obtaining information were interdependent.

Early conferences indicated the need for a broader sampling of practice and of opinions of educational and religious leaders than could be obtained in conferences alone by one person within the time available. Two questionnaires and two opinionnaires were therefore used as supplementary methods of obtaining data. These instruments were designed on the bases of the 1947 report of the Committee on Religion and Education, the problems and issues revealed in conferences, and study of replies to previous inquiries used in this undertaking. In turn, the replies to these instruments were influential on subsequent conferences.

CONFERENCES

In planning the inquiry, it was decided that a primary source of information should be conferences arranged by the Director with responsible educational and religious leaders—principally the former. This decision was based on the exploratory character and limited scope of the inquiry and on the assumption that the judgments of such leaders would be essential both to the effective conduct of this inquiry and to any further studies and experiments, if such should appear to be warranted.

From September 1951 to July 1952 the Director devoted approximately half of his time to individual and group conferences in 85 cities and towns in 33 states representative of all sections of the country. Communities were selected on the bases of responses to the first questionnaire, expressions of interest in the inquiry, what was already known of educational programs, and economical travel schedules. Preliminary correspondence related to the first questionnaire indicated that many local educational leaders would welcome such conferences. A few communities were selected on the assumption that it was desirable to explore the possibilities of developing interest in the problem under study where no interest had been indicated.

In all instances these conferences were arranged by responsible educational leaders in local communities—superintendents of schools, presidents of colleges or universities, deans of schools of education, or chief state school officers—on request of the Director. In order to plan travel schedules, it was often necessary for the Director to indicate that he would be in a given area at a certain time and would be pleased to have a conference arranged, if convenient to the local leader concerned. In very few instances was it necessary to omit conferences proposed by the Director because the time he suggested was inconvenient, or because the local leader did not wish to have the problem discussed in his community.

The Director's purposes in requesting conferences were always indicated in advance as follows: (1) to promote understanding of the aim, character, and procedures of the inquiry; and (2) to seek the judgments of local educational and religious leaders on the problems and issues raised by the inquiry. It was suggested that the local educational leader arranging a conference invite those with whom he wished the Director to confer. Often the Director's suggestions were sought with respect to persons to be invited.

Arrangements for the conferences varied from a brief interview with one educational leader to three full days of carefully scheduled individual and group conferences in one community. In a number of instances the visit of the Director was made the occasion for a meeting of the administrative and supervisory staff of a school system, a meeting of a curriculum or other committee, or a special meeting of the administrative staff of a college or university. In some instances educational and religious leaders from other communities in the area were invited to meet with local leaders. The Director was frequently invited to speak to large groups on some aspect of the inquiry.

The most typical conference, however, was a group of ten to twenty-five local leaders representing the varied educational and religious groups of the community, preceded or followed by a few individual conferences. Most of these group conferences were for a two- or three-hour period. The Director has conferred with more than 2,500 educational and religious leaders, principally the former. This figure is exclusive of large groups where there was little opportunity for discussion.

In each of these conferences the Director was given an opportunity to explain his purposes in requesting a conference; to state the aim, character, and procedures of the inquiry; and to indicate the assistance he desired from the group. The need for cooperation of participants in discovering the problems and issues involved in introducing factual study of religion into the public schools was stressed. After these brief opening remarks the groups participated in an informal manner.

Conferences held during the first three months, principally in Middle Atlantic, Middle Western, and Western states, apart from the opening statements and responses to preliminary questions by the Director, were of this relatively informal character. Whatever seemed important to participants was considered by the group in relation to the context of the total discussion. The Director's role was to answer questions, to listen, and to seek counsel. He assumed this role deliberately as a means of becoming sensitive to the nuances of opinion and attitude. These free discussions tended, however, to exhibit a general pattern.

In almost every group it was necessary to consider first a series of objections to introducing religious subject matter into the schools. Frequently assertions were made that there is and can be no religion in public education without inciting controversy and, as a consequence, increasing suspicion that religious groups are attempting to use the schools to promote their own ends. This defensive attitude was taken by only a small minority, but it usually required about one-fourth of the time allotted to the conference to hear the objectors.

At the first pause, some participant usually differed with this view and indicated by a few illustrations that there is in fact a very real problem which merits careful study. Then the discussions were usually directed to various alternatives. The most frequently suggested alternative was development of moral and spiritual values. Frequently several participants would contend that the public schools should avoid religion but stress moral and spiritual values because there is general agreement that these values are inherent in education, that they are nonsectarian, and, therefore, that the schools are free to do all they can in this area. Usually there was considerable, but seldom unanimous, support for this view.

Almost always someone would raise questions about the effectiveness of moral and spiritual education divorced from any consideration of the role of religion. This usually turned the discussion to a consideration of the possibility of teaching a nonsectarian religion—a common core of religious belief. Here illustrations of what the schools are now doing, or have attempted to do and had to eliminate on account of objections, were often given. This frequently led to a consideration of the rights of the dominant religious group of the community, and sometimes consideration was given to the protection of the religious liberties of minorities. Generally it required about half of the conference period to reach this stage of the discussion.

It was often necessary for the Director to interject questions or statements to bring the discussion to a consideration of the alternative of factual study of religion when and where it is intrinsic to the curriculum. Generally the objectors were first to respond with restatements of obstacles: Is it possible to be objective about religion? Are teachers qualified? Will greater freedom for teachers in discussing religion in the classroom result in indoctrination in their individual religious beliefs? What are the criteria of objectivity with respect to religion? Who will apply them? Is objective study of religion what the people want? Will the people permit objective study of religion?

At this point, if not earlier, a third group usually emerged who rallied to the support of factual study of religion on educational grounds, some on both educational and religious grounds. The discussions generally produced a majority agreeing that factual study of religion in the public schools is desirable if qualified teachers can be found and if the people of local communities will permit it. A majority of the participants agreed that the study of the relation of religion to public education should be pursued until the best solution is found.

By the end of the first three months of conferences it was

evident that these informal discussions were reaching the point of diminishing returns for the Director and the progress of the inquiry. No new problems or issues were being raised. The reactions of participants, the general pattern of discussions, and the consensus of participants in each conference could be predicted with considerable accuracy. Moreover, by this time the preliminary analysis and interpretation of replies of educational leaders to the two questionnaires had been made. It was decided therefore to modify the procedures in subsequent conferences, in the Southern, Middle Western, Middle Atlantic, and Northeastern states.

This was done in three ways. First, the opening statements of the Director included a résumé of his experience in previous conferences and a summary of the replies to the questionnaires. Second, the position of the committee, the alternative of factual study of religion, and the principles for its application in the public schools were made more explicit. Third, participants were invited to focus their discussion on the problems and issues involved in introducing factual study of religion into the public schools.

This did not eliminate consideration of objections, obstacles, and other alternatives, but it tended to bring them into relation to the central aim of the inquiry. The Director assumed a more positive role in raising questions, giving illustrations, and reporting previous discussions. A majority of the participants quickly went to work on practical problems and real issues. The former suspicion of motives and fear of the inquiry were much less frequently expressed. Usually there was a minority who opposed factual study of religion in the schools on various grounds, but in most conferences there was a majority who supported it on educational grounds. The principal issues in these conferences usually concerned the preparation of teachers for the task and the development of community understanding necessary for experimentation.

It was during this second period of conferences that the opinionnaires were submitted to educational and religious leaders. They were designed largely on the bases of the committee's 1947 report, the Director's experience in previous conferences, and the replies to the questionnaires, with a view to testing the Director's interpretation of the opinions of educational and religious leaders. Beginning about the middle of February 1952, copies of the opinionnaires were distributed to conference groups and made the principal focus for discussions. This procedure was effective in sharpening the problems and issues for discussion.

Conferences held after April 1, 1952, gave opportunity for using a preliminary analysis and interpretation of replies to the opinionnaires and testing the Director's interpretation of these replies by the judgments of participants. It was generally agreed that the replies to the opinionnaires revealed a greater readiness on the part of educational and religious leaders to study the place that should be given religion in public education than had been assumed by participants.

Subsequent discussions tended to emphasize next steps in the study process: How can the community understanding necessary for experimentation be developed? What can be done to prepare teachers for this task?

Numerous requests were made for copies of the opinionnaires for use in local communities, and many of the responses of both educational and religious leaders were sent to the office of the Director. It is believed to be significant that these replies paralleled the replies of selected groups described below.

As should be expected, the opinions of participants in the conferences exhibit the same threefold division found in illustrations of practice presented in chapter ii—avoidance of religion, planned religious activities, and factual study of religion.

Further contributions of the conferences to the insights and judgments of the Director will be reflected in the summary of this chapter.

QUESTIONNAIRES AND OPINIONNAIRES

The conferences with educational and religious leaders were supplemented by the use of two different questionnaires and two opinionnaires (really two forms of the same opinionnaire). Each of these was sent to non-overlapping groups, except in the case of the form of the opinionnaire sent to educational leaders. The purposes of these instruments were to extend the sampling of opinions, to sharpen the problems and issues involved in the inquiry, and to provide some quantitative data both for discussion in conferences and for the generalizations made in this report.

It is important to keep in mind the basic purpose, aim, policies, and procedures of this inquiry. Otherwise, the findings and conclusions of this report may lead to misunderstandings. We did not undertake a general survey nor have we attempted a "scientific" study in the sense of precise measurement of attitudes or commitments to action. The methods employed and the instruments used should be appraised, therefore, in relation to the "exploratory" character and "limited" scope of our task, as we conceived it. They were practical means for eliciting much information about practices in dealing with religion and of discovering problems and issues which those educational and religious leaders cooperating in this inquiry think should be taken into account.

Use of these instruments revealed some important weaknesses. If we were to repeat the study, we would modify them in a number of respects. Justification for their use before refinement lies principally in the inexorable limitations of time within which to conduct the inquiry and the limited objectives to be accomplished. On the whole they served well the purposes for which they were designed. Some specific limitations will be noted in appropriate contexts below.

The first questionnaire, comprising four very general questions within the frame of reference of our 1947 report, sought to obtain information on what is now being done about religion in the public schools and in colleges and universities, and what these leaders think the educational institutions can and should do about religion. This questionnaire, while quite open-ended with respect to what respondents might report, was deliberately biased toward factual study of religion. This bias is inherent in the frame of reference, the aim of the inquiry, and the basic purpose for undertaking it. Respondents were encouraged to express themselves freely on any aspect of the inquiry and left entirely free to report what they considered relevant and important. This many did in long letters. Some also submitted copies of articles, speeches, courses of study, and catalogues. From a very large quantity of material, we presented in chapter ii a few brief illustrations of current practice in dealing with religion.

The groups of educational leaders to whom the first questionnaire was sent, how they were selected, and the percentages of replies received from the different groups were indicated at the beginning of chapter ii and therefore need not be repeated here. Table 1 in the Appendix is preceded by a copy of the covering letter and the full questionnaire (see pages 94 and 96). This table is a quantitative summary of methods of dealing with religion in all types of colleges and universities, ranked as to frequency of use as reported by presidents. Table 2 in the Appendix (page 97) represents an attempt on the part of the staff to give a quantitative appraisal of the attitudes of the respondents to the inquiry as a whole.

It is highly significant, we think, that so many educational leaders, for various reasons, are skeptical and even fearful of opening to objective study the question of the function of the public schools in dealing with religion.   This skepticism and fear are reflected, we believe, in the relatively large percentages of different groups who did not reply to the several instruments used in this inquiry.   We reserve this problem for special consideration later in this chapter.   Here we need note only a few facts.   Table 2 (page 97) reveals that 556, or 45 percent, of the 1,233 educational leaders to whom the questionnaire was sent replied.   Of these 556 who replied, 42 percent were definitely and highly favorable to the aim of the inquiry, 38 percent were doubtful, in the sense that they tended to point out the difficulties, and 19 percent were definitely unfavorable.   The percentage of participants in this inquiry who tend to be favorable to its aims increased as more definitive instruments were used, as will be indicated below.   But we do not know what the 55 percent of responsible educational leaders who did not reply think about this problem.

The second questionnaire was deliberately made more explicit with respect to the basic aim of the inquiry.   Early conferences revealed the need for this instrument.   Many participants in these conferences confused the aim of the inquiry with proposals to "teach" religion in the public schools. The four questions were therefore intended to sharpen the focus on factual study of religion when and where it is intrinsic to school experience in contrast with the "teaching" of religion.   A copy of the second questionnaire and a copy of an accompanying statement about the inquiry are reproduced in the Appendix (see pages 97 and 98).   The covering letter was the same as used with the first questionnaire.

This second instrument was sent to all superintendents of public schools in cities under 50,000 in population as listed in the *Educational Directory* published by the Office of Education, Federal Security Agency, and to all professors of education as listed in the membership list of the National Society of College Teachers of Education, none of whom had received the first questionnaire, except in the case of deans of schools of education or heads of departments of education and a few others who were also listed as professors of education. Thus, proportional geographical representation was attained. A total of 3,360 questionnaires were sent to the superintendents and 721 replies were received, or 21 percent of the entire group. Four hundred fifty-six questionnaires were sent to professors of education and 229 replies were received, or 50 percent of the entire group.

Many of the respondents wrote long letters explaining their replies to the four questions, while others indicated their answers on the questionnaire sheet itself and returned it. The questions were designed with a view to quantitative treatment of the replies. Great care was taken to interpret the replies objectively. All replies were analyzed twice, first soon after they were received and second after an interval of several weeks. In case of any doubt about the intent of a respondent with respect to his reply to a particular question, it was appraised as a "qualified" affirmative or negative as the total context of his replies to all four questions appeared to warrant.

Table 3 (page 102) presents a quantitative summary of the replies to the second questionnaire. It will be noted that from 74 to 80 percent of the respondents favor the factual study of religion in the public schools, as against 26 to 20 percent who think that it is undesirable. On the whole the professors of education are more favorable to such study than are the superintendents.

In only one instance did superintendents express greater approval than did the professors of education. This was in reply to the third question: "Do you think it is educationally desirable that the corporate life and teaching of the public schools should stress the *moral imperative* of developing one's own religious faith—convictions and commitments?" Here we think an inadequate phrasing of the question permitted an interpretation not intended, namely, that this meant a moral imperative to believe in a body of religious teaching. The superintendents appear, in greater proportion than the professors of education, to have so interpreted it *with approval.*

A significant difference appears also in replies to question four. This question was different for each group. The question for superintendents was: "Do you think it is possible in your community to increase freedom of inquiry and discussion in this controversial area?" The question sent to professors of education was: "Do you think it is desirable that publicly supported teacher education institutions assist prospective and in-service teachers to teach objectively about religion in the public schools?" The professors of education appeared much more ready to support the preparation of teachers for factual study of religion in the public schools than the superintendents to support increased freedom of inquiry and discussion in this area in their communities. Doubtless this difference is in part a reflection of a theoretical desirability as viewed by the professors and a practical question of feasibility from the point of view of the superintendents.

From 74 to 80 percent of the superintendents and professors replying to the second questionnaire appear to think that factual study of religion is desirable. We believe this is significant. As was indicated above, only 42 percent of the 556 educational leaders replying to the first questionnaire were highly favorable to the aim of the inquiry. These were, of course, reactions of quite different groups to two different instruments. Nonetheless, the replies appear to indicate that making the objectives more explicit increases the percentage of support for factual study of religion in the public schools.

The opinionnaires were designed, in part, to test this hypothesis and to discover what additional problems and issues, if any, should be taken into account.

Two forms of the opinionnaire were thought to be desirable because educational leaders had previously had an opportunity to reply to one of the two questionnaires and therefore presumably knew something about the objectives of the inquiry. Religious leaders, on the other hand, except for approximately 200 who had participated in conferences with the Director, presumably had had no previous orientation to the study. It was therefore decided to state the position of the committee as explicitly as possible in a series of eleven propositions in the form sent to educational leaders. They were requested to reply by checking a five-point scale of agreement and disagreement with this position as revealed by each proposition. It was thought desirable to present these same eleven propositions in the form sent to religious leaders, but to pair each proposition with a second statement intended to be in direct opposition. This was intended to make more explicit the problems and issues involved in factual study of religion in the public schools. The religious leaders were requested to choose the proposition in each pair which most closely approximated their own opinions of what is desirable in the public schools. That in some cases we did not succeed in making these pairs of propositions clearly opposites was revealed by the replies, specific instances of which will be noted below.

The opinionnaires were deliberately and strongly biased toward factual study of religion. They represented an attempt to make as explicit as possible the tentative position of the committee. The freedom of respondents in replying was not limited, however, by the rigid framework of the opinionnaire or the more or less dogmatic statements of the propositions. They were invited to write statements explaining their replies, and many did. The religious leaders were requested to choose between alternative propositions and to explain their choices.

The educational leaders to whom opinionnaires were sent were selected on the basis of the positions they occupy. Each had already had an opportunity to reply to either the first or the second questionnaire, but not all had done so. A total of 2,309 opinionnaires were sent to educational leaders as follows: 48 chief state school officers (26, or 54 percent, replied); 213 superintendents of schools in cities of 50,000 and over in population (88, or 41 percent, replied); 723 superintendents of schools in cities under 50,000 in population (sent only to those who had replied to the second questionnaire; of the 723, 395, or 55 percent, replied); 155 presidents of state or municipal colleges or universities, other than state teachers colleges (69, or 45 percent, replied); 220 presidents of church-related or independent colleges or universities (sent to most of those who had replied to the first questionnaire, not all; of the 220, 118, or 54 percent, replied); 172 presidents of state teachers colleges, or state colleges which formerly were state teachers colleges (76, or 43 percent, replied); 99 deans of schools of education or heads of departments of education in all types of institutions (47, or 48 percent, replied); 489 professors of education in all types of institutions (230, or 47 percent, replied); 190 persons selected by the Director (84, or 41 percent, replied). Thus, of the 2,309 opinionnaires sent to the nine groups of educators, a total of 1,133, or 49 percent, were returned.[1]

The religious leaders were selected on request of the Director of the inquiry by responsible officers in the central offices of the three major faith groups. Special pains were taken to include representatives from all sections of the United

[1] Discrepancies in number of persons included in the different groups as compared with those indicated for the first and second questionnaires are accounted for by corrections in classification, elimination of duplicates, and temporary vacancies in positions.

States. A total of 2,500 opinionnaires were sent to 1,685 Protestants (577, or 34 percent, replied); 434 Roman Catholics (142, or 33 percent, replied); 149 Jews (24, or 16 percent, replied);[2] and 232 persons selected by the Director but unclassified with respect to religious faith (92, or 40 percent, replied). Thus, of 2,500 opinionnaires sent to four groups of religious leaders, a total of 835, or 33 percent, were returned.

Copies of the covering letters, the instructions, the eleven pairs of propositions contained in the opinionnaires, a complete quantitative analysis of the replies of the above groups to each pair of propositions of the opinionnaires, and summaries for the entire set of eleven pairs of propositions are presented in Tables 4–18 in the Appendix.

No significant differences were found among the replies of the nine groups of educators. Detailed analyses of the responses of the several groups are, therefore, not presented in the Appendix. These data are on file in the office of the committee at the American Council on Education and will be supplied to persons particularly interested.

The total of replies of the 1,133 educational leaders saying "I completely agree" and "I agree, with qualifications" constitute from 70 to 89 percent of all replies on the different propositions. On only four propositions, as indicated below, was the agreement less than 83 percent. The total of "I disagree, with qualifications" and "I completely disagree" varied from 3 to 12 percent.

When the four groups of religious leaders are combined (see Tables 17 and 18, pages 122 and 123), it is seen that from 72 to 94 percent chose the proposition which represents the position of the committee. The differences in opinions among the four groups of religious leaders also emphasize the same four propositions on which the educational leaders evidenced

---

[2] The disproportionate response of the Jewish group is discussed later in this chapter.

the lowest percentage of agreement with the position of the committee. The statements of these propositions are now clearly seen to have been inadequate. These propositions require special consideration.

The pair of propositions identified as III-A and B, Table 6 (page 111), was intended to contrast two opposing approaches to a study of the problem—one approach is to defer any experimentation with factual study of religion in the public schools until policy has been firmly adopted by the community (Proposition A); the other is to experiment first to determine what policy to adopt (Proposition B). It is significant, we think, that religious leaders are apparently more ready to approve experimentation than are educational leaders, as indicated by the fact that 83 percent of the combined groups of religious leaders and only 72 percent of all educational leaders chose Proposition B. This difference in opinion appears to emphasize the practical problem faced by educational administrators in contrast to the theoretical desirability of factual study of religion as viewed by the religious leaders. There were marked differences of opinion among the religious leaders as indicated by the fact that 87 percent of the Protestants, 75 percent of the Roman Catholics, and only 42 percent of the Jews chose Proposition B. Both the Protestants and the Roman Catholics appear to be more ready to support experimentation in this area than are educational leaders. The minority status of Jews is doubtless an important factor in determining their opinions with respect to this issue. They appear to think that prior adoption of policy tends to safeguard their religious liberty.

The pair of propositions identified as VI–A and B, Table 9 (page 114), was intended to contrast two opposing assumptions with respect to probable consequences of: (1) teaching moral and spiritual values divorced from consideration of the relation of religion thereto (Proposition A), and (2) factual study of religion in relation to these values (Proposition B). Admittedly, the statement of the propositions did not make the intended opposition entirely clear. Nonetheless, the differences of opinion were marked and, we believe, they indicate fundamental differences in convictions with respect to the issue. The percentages of the various groups favoring Proposition B were as follows: All educational leaders, 70 percent; all religious leaders, 72 percent; Protestants, 79 percent; Roman Catholics, 44 percent; and Jews, 50 percent.

The next pair of propositions requiring special consideration was identified as VII–A and B, Table 10 (page 115). The intent was to contrast the possibilities of obtaining community assent and administrative approval for experimentation with the factual study of religion in the public schools under qualified teachers (Proposition A) with the assumption that no teacher is or can be qualified to guide students in such study (Proposition B). Here, again, the educational leaders appear to be more skeptical than the religious leaders when considered as one group. This, too, is thought to be associated with the practical problems of administration. Unless or until superintendents, and educators in general, are assured of community assent and approval of boards of education, they do not view with favor the responsibility for selecting teachers for this task. Many educators emphasize the danger that other teachers not qualified might undertake such practice. The percentages of the various groups favoring Proposition A were as follows: all educational leaders, 74 percent; all religious leaders, 85 percent; Protestants, 90 percent; Roman Catholics, 77 percent; and Jews, 25 percent.

The final pair of propositions requiring special consideration was identified as X–A and B, Table 13 (page 118). The intent was to contrast what we have designated as "planned religious activities" (Proposition A) with "factual study of religion" (Proposition B) as methods to be employed in the public schools. The statement of these propositions was unfortunately confused by the use of the terms "direct" and "indirect" and by the fact that the two propositions are not necessarily in opposition. Many educational and religious leaders said that they could see a place for both. It is believed, however, that there are fundamental differences of conviction on this issue. The percentages of the various groups favoring Proposition B were as follows: all educational leaders, 74 percent; all religious leaders, 76 percent; Protestants, 83 percent; Roman Catholics, 52 percent; and Jews, 71 percent.

As indicated above there are doubtless fundamental differences in the views of the religious groups with respect to some of the propositions as stated in the opinionnaire. Since we are concerned with what the public schools can and should do about religion on educational grounds, these differences need not be considered further in this report.

The most significant fact revealed by this inquiry is that, with exceptions noted, all groups of educational and religious leaders have strongly supported the position of the committee. This is strikingly revealed in replies to the pair of propositions identified as XI–A and B, Table 14 (page 119). It should be noted that 89 percent of the 1,133 educational leaders, 96 percent of the Protestants, 92 percent of the Roman Catholics, 63 percent of the Jews, and 88 percent of the unidentified mixed group of educational leaders and religious leaders think that the appropriate place of religion in public education requires further study and experimentation. When this fact is considered in relation to the strong support for the position of the committee on most of the other propositions, it would appear that the educational and religious leaders participating in this study are prepared to support further studies and experimentation in this field.

Approximately 7,000 educational leaders and 3,000 religious leaders representative of all sections of the United States and of each of the three major faith groups, were invited to participate in one or more aspects of this inquiry—conferences, replies to questionnaires, replies to opinionnaires, and correspondence. Of these totals, approximately 3,500 educational leaders and 1,000 religious leaders actually participated. As indicated above, the percentages of participation for the different groups varied greatly—from 16 to 64 percent.

Why did so large a proportion of the educational and religious leaders fail to accept the invitation to cooperate in this study? In extenuation of their failure it should be stated that there was no direct follow-up on any of the instruments used. It is probable that the well-known allergy to questionnaire and opinionnaire studies is widespread, particularly when applied to fields such as this which require careful thought before replies are formulated. Some wrote that they had picked up the instruments several times, but on account of the time required to reply had repeatedly laid them aside hoping to find the time to formulate more thoughtful responses later. The more often such tasks are laid aside, the easier it is to conclude that it is too late to be helpful. We believe, however, that the over-all percentage of replies was about what should be expected in a study of this problem.

Two conferences were held with representatives of the principal Jewish organizations of America to discuss the issues involved in factual study of religion in the public schools. It is believed that Jewish religious leaders did not reply to the opinionnaire in as large proportion and did not support the position of the committee as strongly as did Catholics and Protestants because of fear of the possible consequences of such a policy in actual practice. Their hesitancy appears to be based principally on apprehension that such study will not be factual. Christians seeking to understand the historical meaning of this issue to the Jews, who in our society are always a minority and often a very small minority, should be sympathetic to their need for reassurance that their religious liberty will be respected. It is our understanding that Jewish religious leaders are favorable to factual study of religion when and where it is intrinsic to school experience, but are skeptical of the feasibility of attempting more than is unavoidable. With this view many Christians are in agreement. It should be emphasized that the committee's quest is for equal justice to individuals of all religious faiths and of none.

EXCERPTS FROM INTERPRETATIONS OF REPLIES OF EDUCATIONAL AND RELIGIOUS LEADERS TO THE SECOND QUESTIONNAIRE AND THE OPINIONNAIRES

The replies of educational and religious leaders to the questionnaires and opinionnaires tended to fall into the threefold pattern we observed in practice and noted in conferences, namely, *avoidance of religion, planned religious activities,* and *factual study of religion.* It may be helpful at this point to reproduce a few excerpts from interpretations of replies to the second questionnaire and the opinionnaires. The staff and the committee have used their best judgment in classifying these excerpts. It is quite possible that the person writing a particular statement would classify his position differently.

The following excerpts were selected from all the replies to the second questionnaire and to the opinionnaires with a view to presenting a fairly representative picture of the opinions of educational and religious leaders cooperating in this inquiry.

AVOIDANCE OF RELIGION

From superintendents of schools

It may be possible in my community to increase freedom of inquiry and discussion in this controversial area but I do not want to have any part in this leadership. [Small city]

. . . . . .

We now have religion out of the public schools—let's keep it out. [Small city]

. . . . . .

It has been my firm opinion that the religions of today have failed miserably in any justification for their existence and because of this have lost the confidence of the populace. Because of this conviction, I am definitely not favorably inclined toward today's inclusion of religion in education's course of study. [Small city]

. . . . . .

I think it is desirable that students have a more comprehensive knowledge of all religions and be motivated in our schools in developing their own religious faith; but in my experiences, I have found it difficult to do this because of adult opposition. Some attempt to discuss religious beliefs in our social studies classes has met with such criticism that the unit had to be deleted. [High school principal in a small town]

. . . . . .

While we recognize the values of greater understanding concerning religion, the faiths and varying tenets of religious groups, I question the advisability of establishing, at this time, formal approaches in public schools. Teachers should possess these understandings and reflect understanding attitudes in their contacts with children as individuals and groups. [Small town]

. . . . . .

From a professor of education

The best interest of America will be served if you religious education people will just forget about the public schools. Work through the churches.

From a professor of international relations

I think it is highly undesirable for teachers to be given greater freedom to experiment with objective approaches to teaching about religion and religious institutions. My reason is that in practice it will be found almost impossible to find teachers who are qualified to approach this subject with complete objectivity, and when such teachers are found it will be equally difficult to secure the approval of the community for such teaching. I believe we should have a complete divorcement of public education from religion, certainly not from ethics.

From a president of a tax-supported college

My general position is that the schools exist for enlightenment, not for indoctrination nor for any kind of sectarianism. I believe that if the homes and churches do a good enough job of developing and retaining the allegiance to religion of men and women, then the faculties of colleges and universities will be made up of those same men and women, and that they will carry with them, in their scholarship and in their contacts with students, responsibility for religion and will exemplify it.

From religious leaders

I have grave misgivings about the advisability of rushing into a program of teaching about religion in public education. We have neither the staff nor the curricular materials necessary for a satisfactory program. [Jewish]

. . . . . .

We should obey the law. . . . Article I of the constitutional amendments was intended to erect a wall of separation between church and state, and means no public tax money can properly be used to teach religion in the United States. I deplore the tendency to attempt to breach that wall. . . . We have separate privately financed institutions for the teaching of religion according to the ideas of those who support those respective institutions. Why should the schools attempt the function of the churches? . . . As a practical matter the school as now organized is not ready to take over the teaching of religion. . . . If one teaches religion, he has to teach something. There must be content. There is very little content in religion that is not controversial. . . . Released time is a subterfuge. . . . The glory of the American public school system has been its democracy. If we divide pupils into Jewish, Greek Orthodox, Roman Catholic, Fundamentalist, Protestant, Modernist, Christian Scientist, and Mormons, we put obstacles in the way of their social orientation and destroy a desirable unity. [Protestant]

. . . . . .

It must be borne in mind that whether one is willing to face the issue or not, all religion is sectarian. This means that each person holds to certain beliefs and consequent practices and a schedule of acts of worship. The simple fact of the matter is that if one would achieve this attitude of reverence by what is called "an intelligent understanding and appreciation of the historical and contemporary role of religion in human affairs," he would have nothing more than that. For all practical purposes, he would have lost his faith. I am sure that the public schools do not wish to present themselves as enemies of religion.

. . . Religion is not a purely personal affair. It never has been and never will be, any more than chemistry or mathematics are personal. Either they are expressions of truth or they are gross misrepresentations of fact. Tolerance does not consist in the admission that one who contradicts us might possibly be right, but rather in the appreciation of the integrity and sincerity of the *person* who holds the opinion. [Roman Catholic]

PLANNED RELIGIOUS ACTIVITIES

From superintendents of schools

My observation in the past few years leads me to believe there is becoming a feeling on the part of the lay people that it would be wise for schools to emphasize the teaching of morals and to some extent nonsectarian religion in our schools. [Small city]

· · · · · ·

Personally, I believe that the schools might well do a great deal more in the field of religion, but I think it cannot be realized until the authorities of the various religions will get together and agree upon a common body of material which will be acceptable to all, and which will be recognized by their local branches in that light. I think there are many common elements which might be brought together even to the point of preparation of textual or teaching materials, but I am afraid that little can be done unless the various authorities are willing to get together and agree. [Small city]

· · · · · ·

Some way must be found to instill in boys and girls a faith in the Supreme Being, and understanding of spiritual values and their importance to emotional stability, and appreciation for the right of an individual to believe and worship as he pleases. Surely there are some common fundamentals in all religions that can be used and emphasized by various religious groups. Seems to me that we should find these common fundamentals and get together on the teaching of things without sectarian interpretation. [Large city]

From religious leaders

At the present time public schools teach about religion whenever they teach history or study almost any aspect of our present social organization. I believe there is need for greater objectivity in teaching about religion in these fields, especially when treating of revealed religion as opposed to natural religion. . . . The invoking of religious sanctions according to the conviction of the learner might be done through individual personal guidance. To present religious sanctions in a class situation, the school would have to recognize the existence of God and teach the students their obligation to live according to His law. [Roman Catholic]

. . . . . .

Our children are not getting enough religious training in homes and church—homes because of lack of major emphasis, church because of lack of time involved. A study of Bible should be included in school curriculum or at least some form of devotion—could be on a voluntary basis. [Protestant]

. . . . . .

Belief in God as the Creator and as the source of fundamental human rights is something for which our nation will stand until the Declaration of Independence, the Constitution, and the Northwest Ordinance are scrapped. Public schools would be within the framework of the law and in conformity with American tradition were they to teach the fundamental fact that God exists, that man has an obligation of worshiping God, and that there is a natural law knowable by reason. Loyalty, truthfulness, honesty, tolerance, purity, industry, justice, and other virtues can be taught as obligations rather than recommended without any sanctions or proposed as things that are socially desirable or as means of keeping out of jail and of becoming more successful and prosperous. This is an area within which something might be done.

Boyd Bode and many others have taken the position that pupils should be taught and encouraged to develop their own creeds and moral codes. They are to study existing creeds and codes and make their own free selection. In a sense this is true, but not in the sense that one's creed and one's code are to be a synthesis made at will. A Catholic believes that Christ taught what we must believe and what we must do, and that the obligation of the individual is to find and accept the one true faith revealed by Christ. Hence anyone who planned to develop material usable in public schools would have to exercise caution so as to avoid the theory of indifferentism on the one hand and Catholic propaganda on the other. The problem, however, is capable of solution. [Roman Catholic]

. . . . . .

. . . Even though the major religious groups do not agree on doctrine, I believe a common core of beliefs concerning a way of living could be found. If it is truly religion, it will not be merely moral and spiritual values but will help a child to live in accordance with God's plan for the universe. [Protestant]

. . . . . .

Personally I do not think that any one single teacher could ever adequately solve the problem. It seems almost imperative that time should be set apart in the school, and each religious denomination would go to a designated room where the religion course would be taught by one designated by the particular religious sect, and not by some individual appointed by a school board or the like. [Roman Catholic]

. . . . . .

Does some of the problem resolve to this: Is the United States in its founding and principles essentially a Christian country or not? If so, and if it is a land where others are tolerated in a so-called freedom of religion, is there to be no Christianity and Christian principles in our educational life because the others now do not want to be tolerant? [Protestant]

. . . . . .

I agree heartily that religion permeates our culture and is a matter of concern to all our people, that there can be no true education in the full sense of that word when the moral and spiritual values of reality are neglected. At the same time, I believe that the public schools must be neutral on all moral and religious values; otherwise they will violate the religious liberty of some minority group. It seems to me that this dilemma can be solved by including courses on ethics and religion in the curriculum of the public schools. These courses would be taught by official representatives of the various religions who are qualified in the fields of philosophy and sacred sciences. The choice of attending or not attending, as well as the choice of attending this course on the Catholic religion instead of that course taught by a Jewish rabbi, would be left to the individual child and its parents. Thus the religious liberty of all would be protected; no group would be imposing its particular religious beliefs on others; religion and moral values would not be excluded from the public schools. [Roman Catholic]

. . . . . .

It is my conviction that the vast majority of American parents want their children to have a faith in God. The interpretation of God which is given among various religious groups in the United States differs widely. I think, however, that it is altogether possible to find in the great religious literature, especially in the Psalms, expressions of the greatness and righteousness and love of God which could be used as a language of worship in the public schools of the United States without offense to any except the militant atheists or the militant humanists. The children of these groups could be excused from participation in that part of the school's program which affirms the reality, the righteousness, and the goodness of God. For the children of all the rest of the people, it seems to me that such a simple, dignified, classically expressed affirmation could be made both inspiring and meaningful. If this affirmation were prepared by persons who know religious literature, who know the sensitivity of the American people, and who know children, it could be both dignified and beautiful, and could serve as a uniting force rather than as a divisive force in American life—a uniting force which we very desperately need. At the same time, it would give the children the opportunity to learn that to great souls affirmation of faith in God is normal, not pathological! [Protestant]

FACTUAL STUDY OF RELIGION

From superintendents of schools

I sincerely hope that it is possible to increase freedom of inquiry and discussion in this controversial area in the ———— community. I have reasons to believe that such a program might meet with some objection. However, I still feel that it is the duty of the public school to give our boys and girls an opportunity to know the facts as they are recorded in history and give the students an opportunity to think these problems through without fear of intimidation. [Small city]

. . . . . .

Certainly, the omission of references to the influences of religious beliefs upon the course of history leaves serious gaps in any otherwise well-developed social studies course. At present the practice seems to be to mention (perhaps) the advent of Jesus Christ, pass over the Reformation rather hurriedly and gingerly, and discuss briefly the fact that many of the first colonists came to this country to escape religious persecution. For many schools, that is the extent to which we teach about religion. The historical role of religion in human affairs has been neglected, but the contemporary role is usually completely omitted. [Small city]

. . . . . .

Granted that religion is the all-pervasive factor in the learning process instead of a section in the curriculum, it still means that we must re-plan our program to include religion in a comprehensive worth-while way. It certainly cannot gain its rightful position unless it is related to family living, society, and youth. [Large city]

. . . . . .

I believe that only a small minority of our teachers are capable of experimenting objectively in teaching about religion. In the teaching of all areas of education which might be termed controversial, there must be an understanding of the issues by all people in the community. Before teachers attempt to teach about religion, there must be a careful preparation of what is to be taught as well as the where, why, when, and how. A school system and community must combine in that preparation. An in-service training workshop is a prerequisite for the staff and Board of Education members. A state-wide outline of teaching about religion also would be helpful. [Small city]

From professors of education

I wonder whether it would be practical for your committee, together with any competent persons you might want to call in, in addition, to work out two or three usable syllabi that might be used in the public schools. Most of the teachers in the public schools will not be able to take some broad basic ideas and convert them into practical lessons that would be acceptable to the communities in which they teach. . . .

    . . . . . .

Fundamentally, it seems to me that the attitude of the public school toward teaching about religion should be, as has often been suggested, essentially the same as it is toward teaching about various theories of economic and social life. That is, that it should endeavor to make each generation of pupils familiar with the various beliefs and critically evaluate them.

    . . . . . .

I think it is not only desirable but mandatory that teachers in public elementary and secondary schools be given greater freedom to experiment with objective approaches to teaching about religion and religious institutions. . . . If we are to understand the actions and reactions of our neighbors—both next door and across the oceans— we need an understanding of their motivating religious beliefs or denial of them. Too long have the public schools ignored or done poorly their task in this area. Too long have they "read the Bible without comment." Qualified teachers need to assume leadership here as in other areas.

From religious leaders

If our teachers could be trained to deal objectively with other areas of life in which there is controversy, such as economics, political science, or even community mores, it seems that such appreciative objectivity could be achieved in the matter of religion. [Protestant]

    . . . . . .

I should like to say here that where educators are courageous enough to experiment with inter-cultural education, they may also succeed in winning public opinion for broadening the concept of inter-cultural education to include religion. If popular approval of such open discussions and information about the historical religious groups in America can be achieved, we might then be ready for the next step of dealing with religion as a phenomenon of individual experience. [Jewish]

    . . . . . .

Countless opportunities are afforded the well-disposed teacher without forcing religion into teaching. Literature and art are unintelligible without a knowledge and appreciation of the motives which inspired their creators. The history and government of our own country are meaningless unless the religious motives which inspired our country's settlement are understood and unless the basic tenets of our Constitution and the mind of its framers are recognized to be based on religious premises. For example, inalienable rights and equality of men are meaningless unless these properties came from someone who cannot deprive citizens of them. Even in the specific field of religion there are basic truths of our Judeo-Christian background which could be introduced without prejudice to any group. [Roman Catholic]

. . . . . .

I feel that this is a vital matter. Public schools should incorporate knowledge of religion into instruction. The omission of such material ignores one great area of fact and truth that has had a bearing historically in the development of civilization. One cannot study India and ignore the impact that the religions of India have had upon its life and development. The same is true about the history of Western nations.

I see no reason why historical religion, and the Bible as a book, cannot be studied without doctrinal or sectarian bias of interpretation. I believe that pilot or experimental schools might be established to discover and develop the best methods and materials to use. The educators should be encouraged to take the lead, in consultation with religious leaders. This will tend to prevent sectarian bias and will safeguard educational standards.

Of course, the public schools would encourage the students to go to the church of their choice for the theological and emotional interpretation of religion. [Protestant]

. . . . . .

It is obvious, however, that even with all our objections and demands for what is a "qualified teacher," a step in the field of experimentation should be taken. Instead of considering a plan to train in-service teachers in this field, a controlled area should be examined. The in-service recommendation is premature. Why not take trained teachers (teachers who have state teaching credentials, who already are teachers in the public school, and who in addition teach in religious schools) and have them devote three hours a week to an historical study of the three dominant faiths in their social study, history, or any other cognate course that they may teach. This medium can be explored for a year. If at the end of the year it proves satisfactory, it can be tried for another year until it establishes itself. If it presents any complications, the program can be scrapped. This may not be a remedy, but unless an effort is made the present inadequate program cannot be improved. [Jewish]

. . . . . .

We who have worked in the field of religious education and are continuing to work in that field, have been rather vociferous in our demands for the matter of religious teaching in the public school. You have given us an opportunity to be positive in our approach rather than largely negative as we have been in the past. I predict that your study will find a very sincere ally in all of those who work in the field of religious education. I feel that this approach through scientific study and research is the answer. [Protestant]

Summary

The Director is convinced that his sampling of the climate of opinion with respect to the problem of the inquiry was extensive enough to include the entire range from the most extreme opposition to any place for religion in the public school to the most extreme insistence that the public schools should teach a common core of religious belief approved by the dominant religious group of the community. Various types of community in all sections of the country were included. The Director's interpretation of opinions of participants in conferences was supported by the replies to questionnaires and opinionnaires, which, in turn, were supported by judgments of educational and religious leaders in subsequent conferences.

There are, of course, marked contrasts in opinions and practices in local communities and in different sections of the country. These differences were exhibited in all aspects of the inquiry. They appear to be most closely associated with the religious composition of the population and the educational and religious leadership of the local communities. These are factors which should be taken into account in introducing factual study of religion into the public schools. Despite these important differences, illustrations of the entire range of attitudes and practices are to be found in all sections of the country and in most communities. This is doubtless a natural consequence of local control of education and the convictions of local leaders. It is believed highly significant that many leaders in all sections and in most communities think that the present state of affairs with respect to religion and public education is not satisfactory and that the problem should be studied until a satisfactory solution is found.

The reader will want to know how extensively the three different views with respect to the function of the public schools in dealing with religion are held by educational and religious leaders. We cannot answer this question. Wherever our data have warranted, we have indicated our sampling, and deliberate effort has been made to present as representative and comprehensive illustrations as our information justifies. We have found that a majority of those cooperating in the inquiry believe we are on the right track and that the study should be pursued. The fact that there is much confusion and the fact that many are either opposed or skeptical emphasize the need that the study be continued.

We have suggested the alternative of factual study of religion and the principles for its application to a progression of tests. These tests included the very general questions of the first questionnaire, the more explicit questions of the second questionnaire, the very explicit propositions of the opinionnaire, and, concurrently, the very specific consideration of problems and issues in conferences.

From the point of view of developing a plan for pursuing the study of the problem, the reasons for opposition and skepticism are of special concern. Our findings indicate that there are three principal reasons.

First, there are a few who believe that religion is irrelevant, or inconsequential, or even detrimental to human progress. But they cannot consistently oppose free inquiry and empirical methods in any field, and, therefore, cannot continue to oppose factual study of religion if it is demonstrated that it is possible.

Second, there are some who believe that the public schools can and should find a place for planned religious activities and teach a common core of religious belief. They oppose factual study of religion on the ground that it is not enough, or on the ground that teachers and students cannot be objective about religion. The possibilities of their reorientation lie principally in understanding the limitations of the public schools in this area and in convincing evidence that factual study of religion is possible and desirable.

Third, there are many who believe that the public schools must avoid religion on prudential grounds. Most of this group are not really opposed to factual study of religion. Rather they are skeptical that it is possible, or that it will be permitted. This inquiry has clearly demonstrated that all that they need is convincing evidence that it can be done without public controversy and with general satisfaction to teachers, students, and the community.

In the conferences and in replies to questionnaires and opinionnaires two basic questions have overshadowed all other considerations: Can teachers be educated for this task? Will the people permit factual study of religion? In chapter iv we consider the possibilities of educating teachers. We shall not know the prospects for public assent until experiments have been made under conditions which enlist the participation of teachers, students, parents, boards of education, and community leaders.

The data presented in this chapter indicate that many educational and religious leaders are prepared to undertake cooperative studies and experiments to determine the place which should be given religion in public education.   The alternative of factual study of religion and the principles for its application have been strongly supported by the majority of those who have participated in conferences and replied to questionnaires and opinionnaires.

CHAPTER IV

EDUCATION OF TEACHERS
FOR THE TASK

THE central role of the teacher in obtaining community approval for the factual study of religion in the public schools is emphasized by the opinions of those cooperating in this inquiry. In the conferences with educational and religious leaders and in their replies to questionnaires and opinionnaires this concern was stressed above all others. As noted in the previous chapter, the two paramount issues dealt with were community assent and the qualifications of teachers. In the conferences particularly there was very general agreement that public approval is more dependent on the teacher than on any other single influence. If it can be assumed that qualified teachers are available, it is believed that many misgivings will be removed.

It was also generally agreed among those participating in the inquiry that this task requires more personal and professional qualifications than are normally demanded of a teacher. Those opposed to, or skeptical of, the proposal tended to set the standards so high that they appeared to be unattainable. To assume that present teachers indiscriminately should be permitted to undertake the guidance of students in factual study of religion is equally unrealistic. In contemplation of what is desirable and feasible it is imperative, we believe, that the realities of the situation be given due consideration. Among these realities are the very practical problems of sources of teachers, their attitudes toward this problem, and resources for their special preparation for this task.

As a group American public school teachers are broadly representative of the intelligence, values, aspirations, and faiths of our society. They come principally from the middle economic and social groups. They have chosen to enter, at least for a time, an exacting service. The standards of the profession and the public expectations of their service are on the whole conducive to personal growth in desirable social behavior. The public expects conformity to standards which it sets as ideals but largely fails to practice. In a very real sense teachers are of the people they serve, exhibiting the public's strengths to a greater degree than its weaknesses.

We believe that public school teachers on the whole are by choice and necessity better than average middle-class citizens in moral and spiritual values. They are probably also better than average in knowledge and understanding of religion, and in religious convictions and commitments. We have in the present and future teachers of America, therefore, the human potentialities from which must be developed necessary qualifications for the task envisioned.

Furthermore, public school teachers are for the most part products of our public school system. This is particularly true of those in elementary schools and of possibly half of those in secondary schools.[1] If we consider all who have received the major part of their formal education in public schools, colleges, and universities, the contribution of public education to their qualifications for guiding youth in the study and understanding of the role of religion in human affairs is an element of great importance.

This predominance of public education in the preparation of teachers is both an asset and a liability for the task—an asset insofar as their formal education has sensitized them to the conditions under which it must be performed; but a lia-

[1] Current figures are not available. Estimates of those best informed vary from 50 to 60 percent for public secondary school teachers. In some of our cities on the Eastern Seaboard fully 90 percent of secondary school teachers have made all post-secondary preparation in nonpublic institutions, but in the Middle West and West the reverse trend is observed.

bility insofar as their general education has been deficient in knowledge and understanding of the role of religion in human life, particularly if it has conditioned them against consideration of responsibility for the task.

It is true that a minority of teachers in elementary schools and perhaps half of those in secondary schools have received some or all of their formal education in nonpublic schools, colleges, and universities. To this group may be added a small percentage of teachers who have studied religion in tax-supported colleges or universities. In varying degrees, therefore, a minority of the total group of public school teachers may have obtained a more adequate general education, with respect to knowledge and understanding of religion, than public school teachers at large. The findings of this inquiry, however, provide no evidence that more than a very small percentage of them have received any special professional preparation for dealing with religion in the schools.

In all the responses of presidents of colleges and universities only a few indicated sensitivity to the responsibility for special professional preparation of teachers in this area. When this question was put to professors of education and raised in conferences, however, there was quite general agreement on the need for, and the desirability of, such preparation.

Considered from the point of view of the present qualifications of teachers, the task of teacher education for what we propose appears to be colossal. But it does not seem to us to be necessary to wait until a new generation of teachers is adequately prepared for this type of service. Indeed, the reciprocal relationship between theory and practice argues for beginning with the teachers now available in those communities ready to undertake experimentation. Experience in other aspects of education and the American tradition of introducing innovations by experimentation suggest that a solution to this problem may be found in a similar manner.

Fortunately, a considerable number of teachers are to be found in the public schools who, with special preparation and guidance, can be entrusted with this work. Departments of religious education in colleges and universities, both public and private, provide resources in qualified scholars and courses for such preparation. We believe these departments will cooperate with school administrators and teachers in such an undertaking.

In the long view, we believe that both general and professional education for this task should become an integral part of all teacher education. But it does not seem reasonable to expect this to happen until a substantial beginning has been made in school systems, particularly in demonstrating that such practice is desirable and feasible and in creating a demand for qualified teachers. Other innovations in education suggest that the potentialities of in-service education should be carefully considered.

Experimentation appears to be necessary to determine what qualifications teachers must have to guide students in the factual study of religion in the public schools, to discover the problems they will encounter, and to design teacher education curricula to meet their needs. The test of the desirability and feasibility of this innovation should, we think, be made in the classrooms. What happens in the teacher-student, student-parent, and teacher-parent relationships, as a consequence of school experience in this area will in large part determine what is possible. If this experience is mutually satisfying under known conditions, it will then be possible to consider means of establishing these conditions more generally. Teachers colleges and schools of education can then begin to incorporate this knowledge into teacher education curricula.

Teachers engaged in experimental work in this area can make important contributions to teacher education curricula. Individually and collectively they can study the subject matter of their particular areas of competence and service to discover the intrinsic facts and implications of religion which may appropriately be studied by students at given maturity levels. We think this should be done from the point of view of relevance to a fuller understanding of the whole range of subject matter under consideration rather than with the aim of discovering points at which religion can be introduced. Teachers can also describe ways in which they have learned to guide students in such study and define the problems they have encountered in the process.

That teachers will need assistance in these undertakings emphasizes the reciprocal relationship which we think should be developed between teacher education institutions and administrators, supervisors, and teachers. Precedents for this relationship in other aspects of education are well established.

Meantime, it would appear to be consistent with modern educational theory and practice for state departments of education, local school systems, teachers colleges, and schools of education, individually and in cooperation, to enter upon a study of the problem in preparation for future programs. We believe this can be done without undue risks or too great an expenditure of human energy and money. Such exploratory studies should be related to current programs of child development, human relations, intercultural education, citizenship education, and curriculum development. Conferences, seminars, workshops, in-service courses, special summer courses, and the work of special committees are suggested possibilities.

Teachers colleges and schools of education can make important contributions to the exploratory studies and experiments needed. It is believed that their principal contributions should be to the area of professional education—methods and techniques of guiding students in the factual study of religion in the public schools. These contributions are interdependent.

When it has been demonstrated by experiments that factual study of religion is desirable and feasible, the problem of general extension of such practice will arise. If this larger problem is to be solved, the responsibility of teachers colleges and schools of education is clear and twofold: they must provide a well-rounded, fundamental general education in which the study of religion is an integral part; and they must provide specific professional education in the methods and techniques of dealing with religion where it is intrinsic to the curriculum.

Departments of religion, elective courses in religion in other departments, and units on religion in required core courses have an important function in general education. They indicate the concern of the institution for the role of religion in education; they bring to the campus resource specialists in religion; and they provide the means for intensive study of religion. The developments in this direction at the higher education level during the last quarter of a century indicate a constructive beginning in restoring a balance of values and an integrity in higher education. We support this trend as essential to the end in view. It would be a misunderstanding of the meaning of this report, however, if it were assumed that such innovations meet the full responsibility of colleges and universities with respect to the place of religion in general education.

All liberal arts colleges and graduate schools concerned with the education of teachers for the public schools share the responsibility for their general education. It is our conviction that this responsibility cannot be met fully until college and university instructors generally sense their obligation to deal objectively with the facts and implications of religion intrinsic to their fields. It would be unrealistic to assume that this will be accomplished soon, or that nothing can be done until this has been accomplished. But to assume that it will not be accomplished in due time is equally unrealistic. If it is demonstrated that factual study of religion is desirable and feasible, we believe one of the most important consequences will be a growing demand on the part of the American people that it be accomplished.

CHAPTER V

CONCLUSIONS

THE findings of this inquiry strikingly reveal the fact that there is no explicit and generally observed policy or practice with respect to what the public schools and higher educational institutions do about religion. There are in effect three overlapping and confused policies and practices which we have designated as *avoidance of religion, planned religious activities,* and *factual study of religion.* This state of affairs, we think, is a natural consequence of the failure to find a satisfactory solution to a persistent and vital problem.

Avoidance of religion is most frequently and extensively found in communities which are heterogeneous with respect to religious beliefs, or where leaders of minority religious groups have made vigorous and persistent protests against practices of which they disapprove, or where educational leaders have decided to play safe by treating religion as lightly as possible. Planned religious activities are found in all types of community and in all sections of the country, but they are most common and extensive in communities where one religious faith is dominant. Factual study of religion appears to be more closely associated with educational leadership than with the religious composition of the population. We have found examples of this practice—though generally peripheral in character—in all types of community and in all sections of the United States, but only where school administrators have accepted responsibility for leadership in this field. If this generalization is substantiated by further study, particularly by experimentation, it is believed to be of great importance because there would then appear to be the possibility of wide extension of such practice.

We have found little evidence of *deliberate* avoidance of religion, in the sense of a studied attempt to exclude any and all reference to religion, at any level of public education. Contrary to the assumptions of many educational and religious leaders that there is and can be no religion in the tax-supported educational institutions, this study clearly indicates that the schools and higher educational institutions find it necessary to deal with religion in some fashion. Avoidance of responsibility for dealing with religion through neglect or accidental treatment is quite a different matter. It is also at least a debatable question whether or not much that we have classified under the general heading of planned religious activities should be considered an avoidance of the responsibility of the school. To assume that the school is meeting its full responsibility for religious literacy, intelligent understanding of the historical and contemporary role of religion in human affairs, and developing a sense of personal obligation to achieve convictions and commitments, merely by conducting devotional opening exercises, reading the Bible without comment, recitation of prayers, and observance of religious holidays, seems to us to be a misunderstanding of the requirements of a fundamental general education.

Our conviction that the tax-supported schools, colleges, and universities cannot completely avoid religion is abundantly substantiated by actual practice and by the judgments of a preponderant majority of those who have cooperated in making this study. Even those who are most opposed to any deliberate attention to religion in public education admit that it cannot be ignored completely in history, literature, art, and music. It is not strange, therefore, that a variety of attitudes and practices are to be found almost everywhere or that there is no consistent and firm policy or practice anywhere.

We believe it is undesirable, if not impossible, to develop a policy and practice for all aspects of the relation of religion to public education with a view to their application in all communities. To attempt this would be an unwise disregard for American traditions with respect to both religion and education, and of the realities of local situations. Largely for this reason we have deliberately concentrated our thought and efforts on possibilities of developing unifying principles which may be applied to diversities of practice. This has been done in the hope that beacons might be set which will point the way to a democratic solution of this problem.

It would be a misunderstanding of the character and an underestimation of the complexity of the problem, we think, to assume that such a solution can be achieved easily or soon. Religion is too basic to human needs, too vital to man's potentialities, and too fundamental to education to yield to superficial study. But to assume that a solution cannot be achieved is to evidence a lack of faith in the resourcefulness of the American people. A major part of the problem, we think, is the achievement of a fuller understanding on the part of the people at large of the inherent limitations with respect to religion under which the tax-supported educational institutions must operate.

We believe we have found the most promising approach to the further study of this problem, namely, factual study of religion when and where intrinsic to general education. This approach has distinctive merits. It is thoroughly consistent with modern educational theory and practice. It is applicable to any school, college, or university, in addition to, or in substitution for, other practices. Its justification lies principally in the requirements of a fundamental general education. Such practice need not supplant planned religious activities, but it will tend to fill a vacuum caused by avoidance of religion.

Despite the fact that courageous educators are already experimenting with this approach at all levels of public education, particularly at the higher education level, there is insufficient knowledge of what is involved with respect to community approval, teacher preparation, methods, and materials to warrant the adoption of a policy. Most of the experimental tryouts of this practice have been peripheral. So far as we have been able to discover, no tax-supported school, college, or university has yet attacked the central task in any comprehensive fashion, namely, how to deal with the facts and implications of religion intrinsic to all aspects of the curriculum. Until this is successfully accomplished, the problem will remain unsolved.

We do not assume that this approach will receive full and immediate endorsement of the educational and religious leaders of America, much less of the people at large. One more step must be taken, we believe, before educational and religious leaders will commit themselves to so tremendously important a task. This prior step is intensive study and experimentation in a few carefully selected situations, where leadership is ready and conditions are right for a thorough test of the desirability and feasibility of this approach. When such studies and experiments have provided convincing evidence that it can be done, what conditions are requisite for success, and what is involved, it should be the responsibility of the educational and religious leaders of America to commit themselves to the long, difficult task of adult education required for the gradual incorporation of such practice into school, college, and university programs generally. The findings of this study seem to us to warrant the assumption that they will do so.

CHAPTER VI

RECOMMENDATIONS

WE have affirmed our belief that the findings of this inquiry point to a factual study of religion as the best approach to a solution of the problem confronting public education in dealing with religion. Acceptance of this proposal appears to depend largely upon understanding the limitations, with respect to religion, under which the tax-supported educational institutions must operate and the alternatives open to them with respect to aims and methods in this area.

It seems to us improbable, however, that significant progress will be made until conclusive evidence is obtained regarding the desirability and feasibility of factual study of religion. Educational leaders need to know the conditions under which it is possible and what is involved with respect to teacher preparation, methods, and materials, before they can wisely assume responsibility for incorporation of this practice into school programs.

Precedents recently established in the inauguration of other innovations in education are significantly influencing curriculum development and instruction. Studies in child development, teacher education, human relations, intercultural education, citizenship education, and economic education suggest that the problem of the function of the public schools in dealing with religion may be studied most productively in two phases. The first phase should be a limited period of intensive studies and experiments in a few carefully selected situations to discover what is involved, and, insofar as possible, to obtain answers to certain important questions. The second phase is the gradual incorporation of the findings of the first phase into theory and practice generally.

It is to the first phase that the committee feels its efforts should now be directed. If it is conclusively demonstrated that this practice produces generally satisfying results in a few representative communities, the educational profession can wisely assume responsibility for such further activities as may be required. It is assumed that if an adequate plan is developed, certain communities, school systems, and teacher education institutions will welcome the opportunity to participate in such studies and experiments.

In an undertaking of this character it should be understood, of course, that no individual, institution, or community should participate in any aspect of such activities unless or until there is sincere desire to do so. This problem is one which makes peculiarly imperative a scrupulous observance of the constitutional principle of religious liberty. One of the most important aims of such studies and experiments should be to learn how this principle can be applied to all—minorities and majorities alike.

Our recommendations must necessarily be general. We have accepted, on behalf of the American Council on Education, the responsibility for developing a plan which is tentatively called "The Experimental Project." The principal features of this project as now conceived, but necessarily subject to revision in consultation with the Council and cooperating teacher education institutions and school systems, are indicated in the following recommendations:

A. The American Council on Education should develop a plan for an experimental project to include such studies and experiments as may be needed to inquire into the desirability and feasibility of factual study of religion in the public elementary and secondary schools and in teacher education institutions. To make this recommendation more explicit, we propose that the experimental project include the following provisions:

The principal functions of the Council with respect to this project should be: (1) to develop a basic, but flexible plan for studies and experiments in cooperation with selected communities, school systems, and teacher education institutions; (2) to secure the funds required for implementation of this project; and (3) to provide general administration and supervision as needed.

The project should be operative for a limited period, perhaps for three calendar years, exclusive of the time required to make necessary arrangements for its inauguration.

The Council, in consultation with responsible administrators concerned, should select a few teacher education institutions, each of which should select one or more public school systems in its immediate area, for participation in the project. In cooperation with the Council these institutions and school systems should determine the number, character, and scope of particular studies and experiments to be undertaken in the respective situations. Each cooperating institution and school system should, of course, provide adequate administration and supervision for activities related to the project for which it is directly responsible. It may be desirable in some instances for public school systems to work directly with the Council, but we believe the normative policy should be participation through a teacher education institution.

The Council should secure and allocate funds to each teacher education institution and school system participating in the project, as agreed upon, for consultative and secretarial service, conferences, travel expenses, equipment, and materials. It is assumed that teacher education institutions and public school systems will make substantial financial contributions to the project by the participation of administrators, supervisors, and teachers in the actual conduct of studies and experiments.

The cooperating teacher education institutions and school

systems should make the findings of studies and experiments available to the Council for distribution to the educational profession in suitable reports.

The principal objectives of studies and experiments undertaken should be to answer certain questions about the desirability and feasibility of factual study of religion in the public schools and in teacher education institutions, such as the following:

1. In what curriculum areas and at what maturity levels of students is factual study of religion desirable and feasible?
2. What aspects of religion and religious institutions intrinsic to particular curriculum areas are appropriate for factual study at different maturity levels of students?
3. What special preparation do teachers need for guiding students in such study?
4. How can such study be conducted in public schools without offense to minority groups—without infringing the religious liberty of any teacher or student?
5. In what particular curriculum areas and in what aspects of these areas, if any, do teachers and students need additional, or more adequate, materials?
6. What are the criteria for evaluating such study?
   a) For evaluating the judgments of teachers?
   b) For evaluating the judgments of students?
   c) For evaluating the judgments of parents?
   d) For evaluating the judgments of administrators, supervisors, boards of education, and religious leaders?
7. What further studies and experiments are needed, if any, before adoption of policy?

B. The American Council on Education should publish a *News Letter* during the life of the project devoted principally to developments in studies and experiments conducted as part of the project. The objectives of this publication should be to inform persons conducting studies and projects, and others particularly interested, of developments of which they may not have firsthand information; and to present helpful suggestions with respect to special problems, methods, and materials.

C. State departments of education, local school systems, teacher education institutions, and educational associations generally should be studying this problem with a view to preparation for adoption of a policy when it is known what should be done. The following suggestions are made on the assumption that the educational profession should be preparing itself for leadership in this area:

1. A state department of education, a state committee on curriculum development, or a special committee for the study of this particular problem, might undertake a state-wide study of the attitudes and knowledge of teachers at one or more levels of public education with the objectives of obtaining: (*a*) explicit examples of facts and implications of religion intrinsic to teachers' areas of competence; (*b*) how they are now dealing with these facts and implications; (*c*) what problems they have encountered; and (*d*) what assistance they feel they need.

2. A local school system might undertake a cooperative study by educational and religious leaders to discover: (*a*) what is now being done about religion in their schools; (*b*) attitudes and knowledge of teachers with respect to what they are now doing; (*c*) problems teachers have encountered; and (*d*) what assistance they feel they need.

3. A teachers college or school of education might undertake a study of faculty attitudes and knowledge of the problems met with by teachers in dealing with religion in the public schools with the objective of developing appropriate means of assisting prospective and in-service teachers in dealing with these problems.

4. A college or university might undertake a study of faculty attitudes and practices with respect to the facts and implications of religion intrinsic to their respective academic disciplines with the objective of discovering more effective methods of dealing with religion in general education.
5. Individual teachers, or graduate students, under the supervision of competent specialists in colleges or universities, might undertake such studies as the following:
    a) Preparation of a unit of study on the religious institutions of a particular community for incorporation into the social studies program.
    b) Preparation of a guide for teachers of a unit on religion in courses in world history.
    c) Preparation of guides for teachers of literature (American, English, world) for dealing with the facts and implications of religion in relation to selected masterpieces.
    d) Preparation of guides for teachers of art and of music indicating religious elements that may be used to enrich the study of these subjects.

We conclude this report with an appeal to the educational and religious leadership of America. We believe that we have outlined the most promising approach to the solution of this tremendously important problem. But we shall not know unless it is tried. We have attempted to make our proposals and recommendations thoroughly consistent with the best American traditions and with what we believe to be the imperatives of our present situation. Let us therefore commit ourselves to the pursuit of the study of this problem until the best solution is found.

Quantitative Summaries of Replies to Questionnaires and Opinionnaires

Copies of Covering Letters,
Accompanying Statement, Questionnaires,
and Opinionnaires Used in This Inquiry,
and Quantitative Summaries of Replies

Quantitative Summaries of Replies to Questionnaires and Opinionnaires

---

COVERING LETTER SENT WITH FIRST AND SECOND QUESTIONNAIRES

COMMITTEE ON RELIGION AND EDUCATION
AMERICAN COUNCIL ON EDUCATION
1785 MASSACHUSETTS AVENUE, N,W.   WASHINGTON 6, D. C.

COMMITTEE

F. Ernest Johnson, Chairman
Arthur S. Adams, Ex Officio
Homer W. Anderson
Paul J. Braisted
Louis Finkelstein
Jacob Greenberg
John O. Gross
James L. Hanley
Frederick G. Hochwalt
Galen Jones
J. Hillis Miller
John W. Nason
Herbert L. Seamans
Paul H. Vieth
Roscoe L. West

EXPLORATORY PROJECT

An inquiry into the function of the public schools, in their own right and on their own initiative, in assisting youth to have an intelligent understanding of the historical and contemporary role of religion in human affairs.

STAFF

Clarence Linton, Director
Beatrice Hall, Associate Director
Francis J. Brown, Staff Associate
American Council on Education

This is an invitation to cooperate with the Committee on Religion and Education of the American Council on Education in an inquiry defined in the masthead above.

There has been recognition in many quarters of the need for an objective study of the responsibility of school systems and other public educational agencies, including the colleges and universities, for assisting youth to have an intelligent understanding of the role of religion in human affairs. The Committee's 1947 report on *The Relation of Religion to Public Education: The Basic Principles* and the Educational Policies Commission's 1951 report on *Moral and Spiritual Values in the Public Schools* are indicative of the deep interest in the general field which the present inquiry will cover.

The Rockefeller Foundation has made a grant to the American Council on Education for the Committee on Religion and Education for a one-year exploratory inquiry to determine what further studies and actions may be needed should such seem desirable.

Our plan is to proceed selectively by correspondence and field visits. It will be most helpful at this stage if you will write me at your earliest convenience in response to the questions raised on the attached sheet.

Sincerely,

CLARENCE LINTON
Director

The First Questionnaire

The first questionnaire, with a covering letter inviting co-operation in the inquiry, was sent to responsible educational leaders as indicated at the beginning of chapter ii. The questions were as follows:

The following questions are meant to be exploratory. Please respond in any way you wish and raise any additional questions with which you are especially concerned.

1. In what specific ways do the curricula and extraclass activities of your public elementary and secondary schools deal with religion and religious institutions as a part of the culture? (We are concerned with whatever is now being done or planned to assist youth to have an intelligent understanding of the historical and contemporary role of religion in human affairs. *Copies of any reports, proposals, or plans will be appreciated.*) [1]

2. What more do you think could and should be done in the public elementary and secondary schools? (We are concerned with your own interpretation of the situation in the light of factors which you think should be considered.)

3. Is the situation in your community favorable for an exploration of the thinking of educational and religious leaders on the possibility of experimentation in new approaches to objective teaching about the

---

[1] "Institution" was substituted for "public elementary and secondary schools" in the second line of the first and second questions of the form sent to presidents of higher educational institutions.

TABLE 1

METHODS OF DEALING WITH RELIGION RANKED AS TO FREQUENCY OF USE
REPORTED BY PRESIDENTS OF FOUR GROUPS OF INSTITUTIONS
(1 = Method used most frequently)*

METHODS EMPLOYED	RANK OF FREQUENCY OF USE			
	State Teachers Colleges	Other Tax-Supported Institutions	Independent Institutions	Church-Related Institutions
Number of replies analyzed	*80*	*100*	*30*	*70*
Encouragement and facilitation of denominational groups	1	2	7	8
Elective courses in religion	2	1	1	14
Chapel or other religious assemblies	6	8	3	3
Department of religion	12.5	4	2	2
Units on religion in required core courses	4	11	4	10.5
Interfaith council (variously named)	8	7	12	6
Religious Emphasis Week (variously named)	3	5	18.5	7
Chaplain or religious counselor	10	13.5	6	9
Courses in religion in other departments	14.5	6	5	14
Voluntary attendance at chapel or other religious assemblies	7	9	10.5	17.5
Dealing with religion when intrinsic in other courses	17	15	9	4
Religious foundations on or near the campus	5	3	18.5	19
Required courses in religion	....	....	8	1
Cooperation with local churches	9	12	13.5	12
Discouragement of denominational groups	12.5	....	15.5	17.5
Faculty-student committee on religious activities	11	10	13.5	5
Required attendance at chapel or other religious assemblies	....	....	10.5	10.5
Qualifications and attitudes of faculty	14.5	13.5	18.5	14
Religious service of students to churches in local community	17	....	15.5	16
Religious retreat for faculty and students	17	....	18.5	....

* See chapter ii for interpretation of this table and illustrations of practice. The substantive data for this table were obtained from replies to the first question of the first questionnaire used in this inquiry.

role of religion in the culture? [2]   (We are concerned with discovering communities where, on invitation, it may be profitable for me to make a visit, to confer with you and others suggested by you.)

4. Will you kindly write me, at your earliest convenience, setting forth as fully as you wish your own opinions and judgments on any aspect of this inquiry?   (Please send your reply to Professor Clarence Linton, American Council on Education, 1785 Massachusetts Avenue, N.W., Washington 6, D.C.)

CRITERIA FOR EVALUATION OF REPLIES
TO THE FIRST QUESTIONNAIRE

The criteria applied in evaluating the replies to the four questions of the first questionnaire as a whole were as follows:

1. *Favorable to the inquiry* means that the respondent indicated one or more of the following: (1) the inquiry is very important; (2) the situation in the community is favorable for study; (3) the Director is invited to visit the community for a conference; (4) responses to the questions are positive.

2. *Doubtful of the inquiry* means that the respondent indicated one or more of the following: (1) omission of comment about the importance of the inquiry; (2) some question is raised about whether the situation in the community is favorable for study; (3) the Director is not explicitly invited to visit the community for a conference; (4) responses to the questions are equivocal.

3. *Unfavorable to the inquiry* means that the respondent indicated one or more of the following: (1) some statement is made about the risks and dangers in such an inquiry; (2) the situation in the community is unfavorable for study; (3) responses to the questions are generally or specifically negative.

[2] It should be noted that "objective teaching *about* religion" is used in contrast to "teaching religion" or "definite religious instruction" in the questionnaires and opinionnaires. Our report of 1947 used "objective teaching *about* religion" and "objective study of religion" interchangeably. We now believe that "factual study of religion" is preferable because it emphasizes the activity of learners and more clearly differentiates what is intended from "teaching religion."

TABLE 2

REPLIES OF EDUCATIONAL LEADERS TO THE FIRST QUESTIONNAIRE CLASSIFIED
AS FAVORABLE TO THE INQUIRY (*F*), DOUBTFUL (*D*), AND UNFAVORABLE (*U*)*

GROUP	NUMBER OF QUESTIONNAIRES			NUMBER OF REPLIES			PERCENT OF REPLIES		
	Sent	Re-turned	Percent Returned	F	D	U	F	D	U
Chief state school officers.	47	24	*50*	12	11	1	*50*	*46*	*4*
Superintendents of schools in cities over 50,000..............	213	82	*38*	29	31	22	*35*	*38*	*27*
Presidents of state and municipal colleges and universities..........	158	100	*64*	51	30	19	*51*	*30*	*19*
Presidents of independent and church-related colleges and universities.............	547	241	*44*	98	102	41	*41*	*42*	*17*
Presidents of state teachers colleges......	171	80	*47*	33	32	15	*41*	*40*	*19*
Deans of schools of education or heads of departments of education in all types of institutions..........	97	29	*30*	19	5	5	*66*	*17*	*17*
Combination of all groups..............	1,233	556	*45*	242	211	103	*42*	*38*	*19*

* See preceding page for criteria used in evaluating replies to the four questions of the first questionnaire as a whole to obtain the quantitative data for this table.   See chapter ii for illustrations of practice submitted in replies to the first question of the first questionnaire. See chapter iii for an interpretation of this table.

THE SECOND QUESTIONNAIRE [3]

The following questions are intended to be exploratory. Please respond in any way you wish, raising any additional questions, problems, or issues with which you are concerned. Your frank opinions and considered judgments are sincerely desired.   For your further orientation a statement of the genesis, purpose, and procedures of this inquiry is attached.

[3] The covering letter sent with this questionnaire was the same as that used with the first questionnaire. A copy of the accompanying statement referred to in the directions follows.

1. Do you think it is educationally desirable that qualified teachers in the public elementary and secondary schools be given greater freedom to experiment with *objective* approaches to teaching about religion and religious institutions, when and where such teaching is appropriate to the ongoing classroom experience?
2. Do you think it is educationally desirable that teachers and pupils in the public schools seek to learn what Roman Catholics, Jews, and Protestants believe, and why? The major tenets of faith of other peoples?
3. Do you think it is educationally desirable that the corporate life and teaching of the public schools should stress the *moral imperative* of developing one's own religious faith—convictions and commitments?
4. Do you think it is possible in your community to increase freedom of inquiry and discussion in this controversial area? [Sent to superintendents of schools only.]
4. Do you think it is desirable that publicly supported teacher education institutions assist prospective and in-service teachers to teach objectively *about* religion in the public schools? [Sent to professors of education only.]

EXPLORATORY PROJECT
OF THE COMMITTEE ON RELIGION AND EDUCATION

F. Ernest Johnson

On September 1, 1951, Dr. Arthur S. Adams, president of the Council, announced a one-year exploratory research project made possible by a grant from the Rockefeller Foundation to be conducted under the auspices of the Council by its Committee on Religion and Education.

Professor Clarence Linton, on leave from Teachers College, Columbia University, has been appointed director of the project and Miss Beatrice Hall, formerly secretary to the executive officer of several textile mills in North Carolina, has been appointed associate director.

The inception of the present project dates back to 1939, when Dr. Herbert L. Seamans, director of the Commission on Educational Organizations of the National Conference of Christians and Jews, wrote to the late Dr. George F. Zook, then president of the Council, suggesting a study of the relation of religion to public education. This proposal was presented to the Council's Problems and Policies Committee, and subsequently the Council called the Princeton Conference on Religion and Public Education, May 12–14, 1944. The purpose and theme of this conference as stated in a Foreword to the report by Dr. Zook was "to clarify the issues raised in recent discussions of this subject in educational circles, in the press, and in various public and private groups. . . . How to bring about a reconsideration of the relation of religion to education was the central theme of the conference." The American Council on Education published the report, entitled *Religion and Public Education.*

The origin of the Committee on Religion and Education of the American Council is indicated by Dr. Zook in the Foreword to the report of the Princeton conference. He said, "The task of continuing the exploratory work of the conference and formulating a program of further activities in this field has been entrusted by the American Council on Education to its newly formed Committee on Religion and Education."

The committee's report on *The Relation of Religion to Public Education: The Basic Principles* was submitted in 1946 and published by the Council in 1947. The following extracts indicate the deep concern which it is the purpose of the present exploratory research project to pursue.

Certainly the intensified religious concern that is manifest today demands attention by educators. It is part of the complex situation with which education must deal. This is not to say that every particular popular demand must be accepted. Educators may not abdicate their responsibility for leadership in educational matters. This fact often requires resistance to a popular mood for such time as may be required for thinking through a complicated question in democratic fashion. But even if it be assumed that existing conceptions and policies with reference to religion and education call for no changes whatever, that position cannot rest merely on affirmation; it must be supported by fresh reasoning in the light of a changing situation.

It is highly proper, therefore, that all proposals for teaching religion in the schools should be closely scrutinized, for no innovations should come about without benefit of thoughtful criticism. It may well be argued that many proposals for bridging the gap between religion and education are ill-considered and fraught with danger. However, if untenable proposals are here and there advanced and adopted in the field of religious education, they may be in fact a result of an educational policy that has tended to isolate religion from other phases of community life. Nothing elemental in human life can be indefinitely isolated in this fashion. It comes back to protest in unexpected ways. This is happening today in the religious field.

. . . .

The substance of the matter is that contemporary society in America, placing a high value upon education, asks more and more of its schools in terms of curriculum scope and thoroughness, but distinctly less than formerly in terms of final pronouncements on anything. Until this characteristic of education in our time is fully appreciated, the situation must remain anomalous. There are those who think the school program has been too hospitable to newly developed fields of interest. To the modern-minded school administrator this complaint is likely to make little appeal, but it serves to emphasize the current trend. The criterion of acceptance in the curriculum is not universal agreement; rather it may be said that the presumption is in favor of inclusion in the school program of any area of interest that lends itself to objective study if a substantial portion of the constituency of the schools regards it as of vital concern. Educators have shown an impressive breadth of social vision in this respect. We suggest that a consistent adherence to the present-day philosophy of education and a responsible attitude toward their leadership function call for a new and serious approach on the part of educators to the problem of the place to be given to religion in the school program.

. . . .

In the study of the various phases of community life—government, markets, industry, labor, welfare, and the like—there would seem to be no tenable reason for the omission of contemporary religious institutions and practices. Here is an opportunity for a typical social studies project involving observation, interview, and research, and giving firsthand contact with the religious life of the community on the basis of free inquiry. It will in no way commit the school to a particular sectarian position. There are school systems which have used this method, but illustrations of it seem to be very few. It has the advantage of offering pupil initiative and affords an opportunity for independent study. It is not our purpose in this report to propose specific methods to be employed in a social studies program. However, we think that there are large possibilities in it which might be further explored.

. . . .

The intensive cultivation of religion is, and always has been, the function of religious institutions. To create an awareness of its importance is a responsibility of public education. In creating such an awareness the school is but rounding out its educational task, which culminates in the building of durable convictions about the meaning of life and personal commitments based upon them. The school cannot dictate these convictions and commitments, but it can, and should, foster a sense of obligation to achieve them as a supreme moral imperative and to that end bring the students into contact with the spiritual resources of the community.

In 1948 the Department of Classroom Teachers of the National Education Association suggested to the Representative Assembly of the association at its annual meeting that a study group be assigned "to consider the role of the public schools in the development of moral and spiritual values. The recommendation of this study group, that the association develop ways to improve the teaching of moral and spiritual values, was endorsed by the Representative Assembly."

Subsequently the Executive Committee of the association asked the Educational Policies Commission of the National Education Association and the American Association of School Administrators to study the problems and report. The commission's report, entitled *Moral and Spiritual Values in the Public Schools,* was published in February 1951. It is significant that the commission unequivocally states that the public schools can and should teach *about* religion. The following extracts from the section of this report dealing with the responsibility of the public schools to teach about religion are strongly in support of the position taken by the Committee on Religion and Education of the American Council on Education in the report of 1947:

> The public school can teach objectively *about* religion without advocating or teaching any religious creed. To omit from the classroom all references to religion and the institutions of religion is to neglect an important part of American life. Knowledge about religion is essential for a full understanding of our culture, literature, art, history, and current affairs.
>
> That religious beliefs are controversial is not an adequate reason for excluding teaching about religion from the public schools. Economic and social questions are taught and studied in the schools on the very sensible theory that students need to know the issues being faced and to get practice in forming sound judgments. Teaching about religion should be approached in the same spirit. General guides on the teaching of controversial issues may be helpful. If need be, teachers should be provided with special help and information to equip them to teach objectively in this area.
>
> Although the public schools cannot teach denominational beliefs, they can and should teach much useful information about the religious faiths, the important part they have played in establishing the moral and spiritual values of American life, and their role in the story of mankind. The very fact of the variety of religions represented in this country increases the relevance of this suggestion. How many adults could state with reasonable clarity, regardless of agreement or disagreement, what the chief tenets of the various great faiths are? How many non-Catholics know

TABLE 3*

REPLIES TO THE SECOND QUESTIONNAIRE

Question	Groups of Respondents	Affirmative				Negative			
		Yes	Yes-Q†	Total	%	No	No-Q†	Total	%
1. Do you think it is educationally desirable that qualified teachers in the public elementary and secondary schools be given greater freedom to experiment with *objective* approaches to teaching about religion and religious institutions, when and where such teaching is appropriate to the ongoing classroom experience?	Superintendents of schools‡..........	254	300	554	77	121	46	167	23
	Professors of education§..........	71	125	196	86	21	12	33	14
	Combined groups....	325	425	750	79	142	58	200	21
2. Do you think it is educationally desirable that teachers and pupils in the public schools seek to learn what Roman Catholics, Jews, and Protestants believe, and why? The major tenets of faith of other peoples?	Superintendents of schools..........	245	271	516	72	157	48	205	28
	Professors of education..........	78	109	187	82	24	18	42	18
	Combined groups....	323	380	703	74	181	66	247	26
3. Do you think it is educationally desirable that the corporate life and teaching of the public schools should stress the *moral imperative* of developing one's own religious faith—convictions and commitments?	Superintendents of schools..........	351	234	585	81	97	39	136	19
	Professors of education..........	56	116	172	75	26	31	57	25
	Combined groups....	407	350	757	80	123	70	193	20

* See chapter iii for interpretation of this table.
† Qualified reply.
‡ 3,360 questionnaires sent out; 721 replies received; 21 percent replied.
§ 456 questionnaires sent out; 229 replies received; 50 percent replied.

SUMMARIES OF REPLIES 103

TABLE 3* (*Continued*)

Question	Groups of Respondents	Affirmative					Negative			
		Yes	Yes-Q†	Total	%	No	No-Q†	Total	%
4. Do you think it is possible in your community to increase freedom of inquiry and discussion in this controversial area? (Sent to superintendents only.)	Superintendents of schools..........	166	263	429	60	145	147	292	40
4. Do you think it is desirable that publicly supported teacher education institutions assist prospective and in-service teachers to teach objectively about religion in the public schools? (Sent to professors only.)	Professors of education..........	80	113	193	84	22	14	36	16

what a Catholic believes? How many Catholics really know where Protestant views differ from their own? How much do Christians know about what Jews believe or about Jewish religious observances? What are the essential elements of the faith of Islam or of the other major creeds held by the inhabitants of this shrinking world? The unity of our own country, our understanding of the other nations of the world, and respect for the rich religious traditions of all humanity would be enhanced by instruction about religion in the public schools. Like any other teaching in which deep personal emotions are involved, such instruction should, of course, give due consideration to the varying degrees of maturity of the students.

The current facts about the churches and their influence in the United States should also be taught at appropriate points in the social studies curriculum. What, for example, are the principal religious bodies; what are the numbers of their adherents; what legal standing does religion have with respect to taxation, the courts, the Armed Forces? These are matters of obvious civic and social importance; by that token the public schools should teach about them.

For similar reasons, education for international understanding is incomplete, if it does not deal with the influence of different religious beliefs and practices on international relations.

Although study about religion contributes to both the general and the moral education of youth, it should not be regarded by home or by church as a substitute for religious instruction. Our society has made a practical division of labor under which the churches, the homes, and the public schools have shared responsibilities. Building on foundations which should be laid by the church and the home, the public schools shoulder an important part of the task of developing moral and spiritual values. For children who are deprived of religious instruction, either by the negligence or by the considered judgments of their parents, there yet remain other sanctions on which good public schools can build.

The exploratory research project now undertaken by the Committee on Religion and Education is to be an objective inquiry. It is committed to no predetermined conclusions or proposals for action. It is necessarily limited in scope. The study has been described as exploratory and defined thus: *"An inquiry into the function of the public schools in assisting youth to have an intelligent understanding of the historical and contemporary role of religion in human affairs."* By correspondence and field visits the Director and Associate Director, under the supervision of the committee, will proceed selectively to invite the cooperation of educational and religious leaders, members of boards of education, and others, in thinking about what can and should be done by the public schools and higher institutions which prepare teachers.

Special consideration will be given to communities in which the educational and religious leaders think that the situation warrants appraisal of what is now being done and, possibly, planning with respect to what should be done.

The members of the Committee on Religion and Education of the American Council are: [The names of the committee members, which are listed on page ii, followed.]

Inquiries and suggestions should be addressed to Professor Clarence Linton, director, or to Miss Beatrice Hall, associate director, Exploratory project, Committee on Religion and Education, American Council on Education, 1785 Massachusetts Avenue, N.W., Washington 6, D.C.

OPINIONNAIRES

Two opinionnaires, intended to be equivalent, were used. The form sent to educational leaders comprised seventeen propositions representing the tentative position of the committee. Propositions were lettered A through Q. Propositions L through Q were particularizations of Proposition K. These subordinate propositions are omitted in the following tables because they are relevant to further studies and experiments rather than to the opinions of educational leaders on the principal propositions of the opinionnaire.

The form sent to religious leaders contained precisely the same propositions, A through K, sent to educational leaders, with the following modifications in form: (1) each proposition was paired with a proposition intended to be in opposition; (2) each pair was numbered I through XI, and the two propositions of each pair were lettered A and B, the sequence of the propositions representing the tentative position of the committee being irregular, that is, sometimes A and sometimes B; and (3) propositions L through Q were made particularizations of the pair of propositions numbered XI (corresponding to propositions K through Q in the form sent to educational leaders).

We have used the form of the opinionnaire precisely as sent to religious leaders in Tables 4–14 which follow, in order to save space. The proposition in each pair designated as the tentative position of the committee is the proposition which was used in the form of the opinionnaire sent to educational leaders (without the opposing proposition).

COVERING LETTER SENT WITH OPINIONNAIRES

This is an invitation to cooperate with the Committee on Religion and Education of the American Council on Education in an inquiry defined in the masthead above.[4,5]

There has been recognition in many quarters of the need for an objective study of the responsibility of school systems and other public educational agencies, including the colleges and universities, for assisting youth to have an intelligent understanding of the role of religion in human affairs. The Committee's 1947 report on *The Relation of Religion to Public Education: The Basic Principles* and the Educational Policies Commission's 1951 report on *Moral and Spiritual Values in the Public Schools* are indicative of the deep interest in the general field which the present inquiry will cover.

The Rockefeller Foundation has made a grant to the American Council on Education to enable the Committee on Religion and Education to make a one-year exploratory inquiry to determine what further studies and actions may be needed should such seem desirable.

You can help us most effectively at this stage of the inquiry by responding to the enclosed Opinionnaire. We hope you will also submit your over-all judgments on any aspect of the inquiry in a covering letter. A reply by March 1 will be greatly appreciated.

Sincerely,

CLARENCE LINTON
Director

INTRODUCTION TO AND INSTRUCTIONS
FOR USE OF OPINIONNAIRES

INTRODUCTION: This opinionnaire is one aspect of a one-year Exploratory Project defined thus: *"An inquiry into the function of the public*

---

[4] See p. 93 showing the masthead and definition.

[5] In the covering letter sent to Roman Catholic religious leaders, the following sentence was added to the first paragraph: "Monsignor Hochwalt, Secretary General of the National Catholic Educational Association, is a member of the Committee."

schools, in their own right and on their own initiative, in assisting youth to have an intelligent understanding of the historical and contemporary role of religion in human affairs."

The committee has chosen to keep the focus of this inquiry on the function of the public schools in dealing with religion and religious institutions. This study goes beyond moral and spiritual values as generally defined. The committee believes that it is necessary to make explicit the function of the public schools in dealing with religion if the teaching of moral and spiritual values is to be effective.

For purposes of this inquiry "public schools" are defined as elementary schools, high schools, colleges and universities, and professional schools supported principally by public tax funds.

This tentative statement of issues and proposals represents the present thinking of the committee. Before a definite request is made for additional funds for further studies and experimental pilot projects, the committee requests your further cooperating in sharpening the issues and determining the most feasible proposals for further studies and projects.

INSTRUCTIONS: Please read the entire statement before responding to any of the lettered paragraphs, then start with paragraph *A* and continue with each paragraph in the order presented, indicating the degree of your agreement or disagreement by circling the appropriate number preceding the capital letter in the left margin, interpreted as follows:

1—I completely agree
2—I agree, with qualifications
3—I am undecided
4—I disagree, with qualifications
5—I completely disagree

You may reproduce this tentative statement of issues and proposals for use of groups or individuals; or, if you prefer, additional copies will be supplied promptly.

The introduction to the opinionnaire submitted to religious leaders was the same as that submitted to educational leaders. The instructions were as follows:

INSTRUCTIONS: This opinionnaire presents eleven pairs of propositions; the first pair is numbered I-*A* and *B*, the second pair is numbered II-*A* and *B*, etc. All the propositions are related to what the public schools can and should do about religion. The two propositions in each pair are intended to present opposing points of view. *Please read both propositions of each pair.* You may not agree completely with either proposition. Choose the proposition which most nearly approximates your own opinion and circle the letter in the left margin which designates the proposition chosen. We would also welcome any notes you may wish to make in the margin as an elaboration of your opinion on each proposition.

The opinionnaire has been designed for use by groups as well as individuals. You may reproduce it for use by groups or individuals as you wish; or, if you prefer, additional copies will be supplied promptly. Ministerial associations, school staffs, and other groups may wish to study and discuss the opinionnaire as a whole before responding to each of the pairs of propositions in turn. *In cases of use by groups, it is requested that the number of persons choosing each proposition be written in the margin preceding the letter designating the proposition chosen.*

THE FIRST PAIR OF PROPOSITIONS

I–A The constitutional principle of religious liberty (First Amendment to the Constitution of the United States) and the tradition of separation of Church and State were never intended to mean and do not now mean that the public schools have no function in dealing with religion. The public schools cannot ignore religion; no basic institution or influence in life can be indefinitely excluded from these schools. Since religion permeates our culture and is a matter of concern to all our people, whatever their religious beliefs, the public schools must deal with religion. The basic issues, therefore, are Why? What? How? When? Who? There is need for a restudy of the function of public schools in dealing with religion. At present there is no clear-cut and generally approved policy to guide boards of education, administrators, and teachers. As a consequence there is much confusion in thinking and practice.

B The American people have decided the issue of the function of the public schools in dealing with religion. The long-established constitutional principle of religious liberty (First Amendment to the Constitution of the United States) and the tradition of separation of church and state are approved by most of the people. The public schools must be neutral on all religious matters; otherwise they will violate the religious liberty of some minority group. Teaching religion is the function of home, church, and special agencies for religious education. Whenever questions about religion arise in the public schools they should be referred to the home or church; they are not the concern of the public school. There is, therefore, no problem and no need for a restudy of the function of the public schools in dealing with religion.

TABLE 4: Opinions of Educational and Religious Leaders*

Opinions of Groups by Classifications	Number	Percent
Opinions of 1,133 educational leaders on Proposition A:†		
1. I completely agree................................	759	67
2. I agree, with qualifications.....................	235	21
Total of 1 and 2................................	*994*	*88*
3. I am undecided...................................	17	2
4. I disagree, with qualifications..................	37	3
5. I completely disagree............................	29	3
Total of 4 and 5................................	*66*	*6*
Reply was not usable...............................	56	5
Opinions of 835 religious leaders:‡		
Choosing Proposition A.............................	774	94
Choosing Proposition B.............................	42	5
Reply was not usable...............................	19	2

* Proposition A represents the tentative position of the committee.
† 2,309 opinionnaires were sent out; 1,133 replies received; 49 percent.
‡ 2,500 opinionnaires were sent out; 835 replies received; 33 percent.

THE SECOND PAIR OF PROPOSITIONS

II–A Leadership for restudy of the function of the public schools in dealing with religion should come from religious leaders. Initiative on the part of educators in inviting cooperative study of this problem will result in controversy which will do more harm than good. One of the first steps should be for religious leaders to agree on policy and procedures acceptable to educators and the citizens of communities.

B Educators should invite religious leaders and lay citizens to cooperate in a restudy of the function of the public schools in dealing with religion. The justifiable function of public schools in dealing with religion is a matter of educational policy and procedure, responsibility for which is shared by home, church, school, and other agencies; but educators may not abdicate their responsibility for leadership in educational matters.

TABLE 5: OPINIONS OF EDUCATIONAL AND RELIGIOUS LEADERS*

Opinions of Groups by Classifications	Number	Percent
Opinions of 1,133 educational leaders on Proposition B:†		
1. I completely agree	683	60
2. I agree, with qualifications	283	25
Total of 1 and 2	*966*	*85*
3. I am undecided	43	4
4. I disagree, with qualifications	39	3
5. I completely disagree	31	3
Total of 4 and 5	*70*	*6*
Reply was not usable	54	5
Opinions of 835 religious leaders:‡		
Choosing Proposition B	723	87
Choosing Proposition A	77	9
Reply was not usable	35	4

* Proposition B represents the tentative position of the committee.
† 2,309 opinionnaires were sent out; 1,133 replies received; 49 percent.
‡ 2,500 opinionnaires were sent out; 835 replies received; 33 percent.

THE THIRD PAIR OF PROPOSITIONS

III–A In view of the differences in points of view with regard to the
justifiable function of the public schools in dealing with religion,
it is necessary to obtain agreement of the representatives of all concerned
before innovations in practice are introduced. Firm policy and definite
procedures should be agreed to prior to any innovations in the public schools.

B It is not necessary to await agreement on firm policy and definite
procedures before the public schools undertake experimental projects
designed to discover the most effective ways to deal with religion. Wisdom
in the public relations of the public schools requires that all concerned have
an opportunity, through their representatives, to participate in the study of
the problem. Assent will be given for innovations in practice more readily
if continuous study and evaluation of such innovations are assured prior to
the adoption of policy.

TABLE 6: Opinions of Educational and Religious Leaders*

Opinions of Groups by Classifications	Number	Percent
Opinions of 1,133 educational leaders on Proposition B:†		
1. I completely agree	474	42
2. I agree, with qualifications	344	30
Total of 1 and 2	*818*	*72*
3. I am undecided	114	10
4. I disagree, with qualifications	79	7
5. I completely disagree	58	5
Total of 4 and 5	*137*	*12*
Reply was not usable	64	6
Opinions of 835 religious leaders:‡		
Choosing Proposition B	693	83
Choosing Proposition A	113	13
Reply was not usable	29	4

* Proposition B represents the tentative position of the committee.
† 2,309 opinionnaires were sent out; 1,133 replies received; 49 percent.
‡ 2,500 opinionnaires were sent out; 835 replies received; 33 percent.

THE FOURTH PAIR OF PROPOSITIONS

IV–A   Since the American people support and control the public schools, it is to the people that educational and religious leaders must appeal for approval of policy on what these schools can and should do about religion. Within the limitations of federal and state provisions, policies and practices with regard to religion in a local school unit are dependent on general assent of the people of that community.   Religious liberty, however, requires that policies and practices of all local school units protect the rights of conscience of all minority groups.   But no group has the right either to impose its particular religious beliefs on or to exclude religion from the public schools. The justifiable function of the public schools in dealing with religion, therefore, must be found in a context which protects the religious liberty of all.

B   Since the people of a local school unit control and support their own public schools, within the limits of federal and state provisions, by majority assent they may legitimately exclude all religious references from the curricula of these schools as a means of protecting the religious liberty of all.

TABLE 7: Opinions of Educational and Religious Leaders*

Opinions of Groups by Classifications	Number	Percent
Opinions of 1,133 educational leaders on Proposition A:†		
1. I completely agree..............................	761	67
2. I agree, with qualifications......................	214	19
Total of 1 and 2..............................	*975*	*86*
3. I am undecided................................	43	4
4. I disagree, with qualifications..................	36	3
5. I completely disagree.........................	16	1
Total of 4 and 5..............................	*52*	*5*
Reply was not usable.........................	63	6
Opinions of 835 religious leaders:‡		
Choosing Proposition A.........................	761	91
Choosing Proposition B.........................	29	4
Reply was not usable...........................	45	5

* Proposition A represents the tentative position of the committee.
† 2,309 opinionnaires were sent out; 1,133 replies received; 49 percent.
‡ 2,500 opinionnaires were sent out; 835 replies received; 33 percent.

THE FIFTH PAIR OF PROPOSITIONS

V–A Since there is no immediate prospect of agreement among the major religious groups on a view of religion or on a religious subject matter which the public schools can teach, these schools must exclude religion, insofar as possible, and invoke exclusively social sanctions for moral-ethical conduct. There is general agreement that home, church, school, and other agencies share responsibility for the formation of character. The public schools can and should teach moral and spiritual values, without religious sanctions.

B While there is no immediate prospect of agreement among the major religious groups on a view of religion or on a religious subject matter which the public schools can teach, there is nonetheless a possibility of increasing agreement on a *quest* for *objectivity* in teaching *about* religion when and where it is inherent in the life of these schools. This possibility is inherent in certain functions now accorded public schools; positive contributions to the formation of moral-ethical character; development of capacity for intelligent action; freedom of inquiry, study, and discussion, within the competence of teachers and the maturity and capacities of learners; invoking sanctions for moral-ethical conduct consistent with the conscience of individual teachers and learners.

TABLE 8: Opinions of Educational and Religious Leaders*

Opinions of Groups by Classifications	Number	Percent
Opinions of 1,133 educational leaders on Proposition B:†		
1. I completely agree............................	660	58
2. I agree, with qualifications.....................	278	25
Total of 1 and 2.............................	*938*	*83*
3. I am undecided.............................	52	5
4. I disagree, with qualifications..................	30	3
5. I completely disagree.........................	16	1
Total of 4 and 5.............................	*46*	*4*
Reply was not usable...........................	97	9
Opinions of 835 religious leaders:‡		
Choosing Proposition B.........................	751	90
Choosing Proposition A.........................	44	5
Reply was not usable...........................	40	5

* Proposition B represents the tentative position of the committee.
† 2,309 opinionnaires were sent out; 1,133 replies received; 49 percent.
‡ 2,500 opinionnaires were sent out; 835 replies received; 33 percent.

THE SIXTH PAIR OF PROPOSITIONS

VI–A If the public schools invoke exclusively social sanctions for moral and spiritual values, the consequences will be: inadequate general education; increase in religious illiteracy; relegation of religion to an unimportant role in human affairs, as viewed by the learner; and encouragement of a secular view of life.

B Assuming the possibility of sufficient agreement to permit experimental tryouts of a *quest* for *objectivity* in teaching the historical and contemporary role of religion in human affairs, the consequences will be: teachers and pupils will grow in their capacity to be objective; freedom of conscience of teachers and pupils will be increasingly protected because indoctrination in any religious, non-religious, or anti-religious view will be equally inconsistent; religious and/or social sanctions will be invoked according to individual convictions and commitments; and religious literacy will be increased.

TABLE 9: Opinions of Educational and Religious Leaders*

Opinions of Groups by Classifications	Number	Percent
Opinions of 1,133 educational leaders on Proposition B:†		
1. I completely agree	424	37
2. I agree, with qualifications	373	33
Total of 1 and 2	797	70
3. I am undecided	168	15
4. I disagree, with qualifications	46	4
5. I completely disagree	28	2
Total of 4 and 5	74	7
Reply was not usable	94	8
Opinions of 835 religious leaders:‡		
Choosing Proposition B	599	72
Choosing Proposition A	128	15
Reply was not usable	108	13

* Proposition B represents the tentative position of the committee.
† 2,309 opinionnaires were sent out; 1,133 replies received; 49 percent.
‡ 2,500 opinionnaires were sent out; 835 replies received; 33 percent.

THE SEVENTH PAIR OF PROPOSITIONS

VII–A The competence of the teacher is the basic problem in obtaining community and administrative approval for experimental tryouts of the *quest* for *objectivity* in teaching *about* religion. Adequate pre-service and in-service education will be prerequisite. It is neither possible nor desirable, however, that any teacher be completely objective. Consciously or unconsciously the convictions and commitments of the teacher will show through his life and teaching. It is to be preferred that his convictions and commitments, whatever they are, be avowed, provided the occasion is appropriate and equal rights and obligations are accorded learners. Tolerance of community, parents, and learners will be great when sincerity of purpose, courage of convictions, and integrity of commitments are evident.

B No combination of pre-service and in-service education will qualify any teacher to be sufficiently objective in teaching about religion to protect the religious liberty of learners. Consciously or unconsciously the teacher will indoctrinate learners in a particular belief. In the public schools, the convictions and commitments of teachers and learners are strictly personal affairs. Keeping religion a purely personal affair will continue the tolerance and good will that has characterized public education.

TABLE 10: Opinions of Educational and Religious Leaders*

Opinions of Groups by Classifications	Number	Percent
Opinions of 1,133 educational leaders on Proposition A:†		
1. I completely agree	468	41
2. I agree, with qualifications	371	33
Total of 1 and 2	*839*	*74*
3. I am undecided	92	8
4. I disagree, with qualifications	71	6
5. I completely disagree	38	3
Total of 4 and 5	*109*	*10*
Reply was not usable	93	8
Opinions of 835 religious leaders:‡		
Choosing Proposition A	706	85
Choosing Proposition B	66	8
Reply was not usable	63	7

* Proposition A represents the tentative position of the committee.
† 2,309 opinionnaires were sent out; 1,133 replies received; 49 percent.
‡ 2,500 opinionnaires were sent out; 835 replies received; 33 percent.

THE EIGHTH PAIR OF PROPOSITIONS

VIII–A It is the responsibility of home and church to nurture religious faith. There is an appropriate differentiation of functions among home, church, and public school. All are concerned with the same children and youth, but the public school has been developed to supplement the home and church, particularly in teaching skills, knowledge, and attitudes necessary for effective citizenship. This differentiation of functions is made mandatory on the public school by the constitutional principle of religious liberty and the tradition of separation of church and state. Among the responsibilities of the public school are the nurture of capacity for intelligent action, the teaching of moral and spiritual values, and the formation of moral-ethical character. But the public school must be strictly neutral with regard to religious sanctions for values and character.

B It is the responsibility of home and church to nurture religious faith. The public school shares responsibility with home and church in developing the awareness of the importance of religion in human affairs. While the public school cannot legitimately teach a religious belief, a non-religious belief, or an anti-religious belief, or invoke exclusively religious sanctions for values and character, it can and should invoke the moral imperative that each individual, within the limits of his maturity and capacity, must assume responsibility for developing progressively convictions and commitments by which he will strive to live. No normal person seeking integration of personality and maturity of mind can wish to escape this imperative. The public school can and should infuse its life with this imperative. The application of this transcendent principle protects the religious liberty of atheist and believer alike. Each must assume responsibility for the convictions and commitments by which he strives to live.

TABLE 11: Opinions of Educational and Religious Leaders*

Opinions of Groups by Classifications	Number	Percent
Opinions of 1,133 educational leaders on Proposition B:†		
1. I completely agree	786	69
2. I agree, with qualifications	202	18
Total of 1 and 2	*988*	*87*
3. I am undecided	21	2
4. I disagree, with qualifications	25	2
5. I completely disagree	15	1
Total of 4 and 5	*40*	*4*
Reply was not usable	84	7
Opinions of 835 religious leaders:‡		
Choosing Proposition B	747	89
Choosing Proposition A	35	4
Reply was not usable	53	6

* Proposition B represents the tentative position of the committee.
† 2,309 opinionnaires were sent out; 1,133 replies received; 49 percent.
‡ 2,500 opinionnaires were sent out; 835 replies received; 33 percent.

THE NINTH PAIR OF PROPOSITIONS

IX–A If this moral imperative—that each individual must, within the limits of his maturity and capacity, accept responsibility for achieving progressively convictions and commitments by which he will strive to live —is effectively infused into the life of the public school, the following consequences may be expected: integrity of human relations will be strengthened; learners will join teachers in the quest of the inquiring mind; all the activities of the school will become increasingly significant; formation of moral-ethical character will be promoted; and creative thinking through consideration of diverse points of view will be encouraged.

B If this moral imperative—that each individual must, within the limits of his maturity and capacity, accept responsibility for achieving progressively convictions and commitments by which he will strive to live —is effectively infused into the life of the public school, the following consequences may be expected: the integrity of human relations will be weakened; teachers will indoctrinate learners in their own particular beliefs; freedom of inquiry, study, and discussion will be restricted; the state will impose, through the public schools, an orthodoxy of moral-ethical precepts; religious liberty will be sacrificed for conformity to the dogma of the school; and creative contributions to the culture will be minimized by coercive social pressure for standardization behavior.

TABLE 12: OPINIONS OF EDUCATIONAL AND RELIGIOUS LEADERS*

Opinions of Groups by Classifications	Number	Percent
Opinions of 1,133 educational leaders on Proposition A:†		
1. I completely agree.	546	48
2. I agree, with qualifications.	391	35
Total of 1 and 2.	*937*	*83*
3. I am undecided.	94	8
4. I disagree, with qualifications.	20	2
5. I completely disagree.	19	2
Total of 4 and 5.	*39*	*3*
Reply was not usable.	63	6
Opinions of 835 religious leaders:‡		
Choosing Proposition A.	771	92
Choosing Proposition B.	13	2
Reply was not usable.	51	6

* Proposition A represents the tentative position of the committee.
† 2,309 opinionnaires were sent out; 1,133 replies received; 49 percent.
‡ 2,500 opinionnaires were sent out; 835 replies received; 33 percent.

THE TENTH PAIR OF PROPOSITIONS

X-A The most effective and appropriate methods for use in the public schools in assisting children and youth to have an intelligent understanding and appreciation of the historical and contemporary role of religion in human affairs are direct and specific, such as: reading the Bible without comment and nonsectarian or silent prayers in devotional opening exercises; and teaching a belief in God. Such methods may be used to dramatize the role of religion in human affairs and to create an attitude of reverence.

B The most effective and appropriate methods for use in the public schools in assisting children and youth to have an intelligent understanding and appreciation of the historical and contemporary role of religion in human affairs are indirect, from the point of view of the learner, integral to the life of the school, and infused into all human relations of the school. Direct, specific, and dramatic methods (such as listed in X-A above) may also have an appropriate place, but they should not be relied upon as the basic means of achieving convictions and commitments.

TABLE 13: Opinions of Educational and Religious Leaders*

Opinions of Groups by Classifications	Number	Percent
Opinions of 1,133 educational leaders on Proposition B:†		
1. I completely agree..........................	517	46
2. I agree, with qualifications......................	325	29
Total of 1 and 2..............................	*842*	*74*
3. I am undecided..............................	110	10
4. I disagree, with qualifications...................	82	7
5. I completely disagree........................	36	3
Total of 4 and 5..............................	*118*	*10*
Reply was not usable...........................	63	6
Opinions of 835 religious leaders:‡		
Choosing Proposition B..........................	635	76
Choosing Proposition A..........................	145	17
Reply was not usable...........................	55	7

* Proposition B represents the tentative position of the committee.
† 2,309 opinionnaires were sent out; 1,133 replies received; 49 percent.
‡ 2,500 opinionnaires were sent out; 835 replies received; 33 percent.

THE ELEVENTH PAIR OF PROPOSITIONS

XI–A The alternatives among the preceding propositions which I think are most appropriate for the public schools will require further study and experimentation. There is special need for: an information service; workshops; guides for teachers; studies of experiences appropriate for the various maturity levels in the different subject fields; studies of teaching and learning materials; and the designing of experimental projects with a view to evaluation.

B The alternatives among the preceding propositions which I think are most appropriate for the public schools require no further study or experimentation. The state departments of education, teacher education institutions, and the public school systems are qualified and equipped to do all that is desirable. The public schools are now doing all they should do about religion.

TABLE 14: Opinions of Educational and Religious Leaders*

Opinions of Groups by Classifications	Number	Percent
Opinions of 1,133 educational leaders on Proposition A:†		
1. I completely agree............................	882	79
2. I agree, with qualifications.....................	117	10
Total of 1 and 2............................	*999*	*89*
3. I am undecided.............................	37	3
4. I disagree, with qualifications..................	19	2
5. I completely disagree.........................	14	1
Total of 4 and 5............................	*33*	*3*
Reply was not usable...........................	64	6
Opinions of 835 religious leaders:‡		
Choosing Proposition A.........................	782	94
Choosing Proposition B.........................	15	2
Reply was not usable...........................	38	4

* Proposition A represents the tentative position of the committee.
† 2,309 opinionnaires were sent out; 1,133 replies received; 49 percent.
‡ 2,500 opinionnaires were sent out; 835 replies received; 33 percent.

TABLE 15

SUMMARY OF OPINIONS OF 1,133 EDUCATIONAL LEADERS ON THE ELEVEN
PROPOSITIONS STATED IN THE OPINIONNAIRE AS REPRESENTING
THE TENTATIVE POSITION OF THE COMMITTEE, EXPRESSED BY
NUMBER AND DEGREES OF AGREEMENT-DISAGREEMENT*

PROPOSITION	NUMBER IN AGREEMENT–DISAGREEMENT†							
	1	2	Total 1 & 2	3	4	5	Total 4 & 5	NU
I–A‡.............	759	235	994	17	37	29	66	56
II–B.............	683	283	966	43	39	31	70	54
III–B............	474	344	818	114	79	58	137	64
IV–A............	761	214	975	43	36	16	52	63
V–B.............	660	278	938	52	30	16	46	97
VI–B............	424	373	797	168	46	28	74	94
VII–A...........	468	371	839	92	71	38	109	93
VIII–B..........	786	202	988	21	25	15	40	84
IX–A............	546	391	937	94	20	19	39	63
X–B.............	517	325	842	110	82	36	118	63
XI–A............	882	117	999	37	19	14	33	64

* 2,309 opinionnaires were sent out; 1,133 replies received; 49 percent.
† *Code:*
    1 = I completely agree
    2 = I agree, with qualifications
    3 = I am undecided
    4 = I disagree, with qualifications
    5 = I completely disagree
    NU = Reply was not usable
‡ See Tables 4–14 for statement of the propositions.   There were no significant differences in
the opinions of different groups of educational leaders.

TABLE 16

SUMMARY OF OPINIONS OF 1,133 EDUCATIONAL LEADERS ON THE ELEVEN
PROPOSITIONS STATED IN THE OPINIONNAIRE AS REPRESENTING
THE TENTATIVE POSITION OF THE COMMITTEE EXPRESSED BY
PERCENTAGES AND DEGREES OF AGREEMENT–DISAGREEMENT*

PROPOSITION	PERCENTAGES OF AGREEMENT–DISAGREEMENT†							
	1	2	Total 1 & 2	3	4	5	Total 4 & 5	NU
I–A‡	67	21	88	2	3	3	6	5
II–B	60	25	85	4	3	3	6	5
III–B	42	30	72	10	7	5	12	6
IV–A	67	19	86	4	3	1	5	6
V–B	58	25	83	5	3	1	4	9
VI–B	37	33	70	15	4	2	7	8
VII–A	41	33	74	8	6	3	10	8
VIII–B	69	18	87	2	2	1	4	7
IX–A	48	35	83	8	2	2	3	6
X–B	46	29	74	10	7	3	10	6
XI–A	79	10	89	3	2	1	3	6

* 2,309 opinionnaires were sent out; 1,133 replies received; 49 percent.
† *Code:*
    1=I completely agree
    2=I agree, with qualifications
    3=I am undecided
    4=I disagree, with qualifications
    5=I completely disagree
    NU=Reply was not usable
‡ See Tables 4–14 for statement of propositions. There were no significant differences in the opinions of different groups of educational leaders.

TABLE 17

SUMMARY OF OPINIONS OF 835 RELIGIOUS LEADERS ON THE ELEVEN PAIRS OF PROPOSITIONS STATED IN THE OPINION-NAIRE INDICATING NUMBER OF EACH MAJOR FAITH GROUP CHOOSING PROPOSITION FROM EACH PAIR REPRESENTING TENTATIVE POSITION OF THE COMMITTEE AND NUMBER CHOOSING PROPOSITION IN EACH PAIR INTENDED TO BE IN OPPOSITION

Proposition	Number Choosing Proposition Representing Tentative Position of the Committee					Number Choosing Proposition Intended To Be in Opposition					Number of Replies Not Usable				
	1*	2	3	4	5	1	2	3	4	5	1	2	3	4	5
I-A†	547	138	7	82	774	20	1	16	5	42	10	3	1	5	19
II-B†	511	118	14	80	723	47	19	6	5	77	19	5	4	7	35
III-B†	502	107	10	74	693	60	30	12	11	113	15	5	2	7	29
IV-A†	554	128	4	75	761	7	3	13	6	29	16	11	7	11	45
V-B†	542	122	9	78	751	20	5	12	7	44	15	11	3	7	40
VI-B†	458	62	12	67	599	65	54	2	7	128	54	26	10	18	108
VII-A†	514	109	6	77	706	29	16	15	6	66	34	17	3	9	63
VIII-B†	532	118	15	82	747	17	6	8	4	35	28	18	1	6	53
IX-A†	556	122	14	79	771	3	3	1	2	13	18	17	5	11	51
X-B†	478	74	17	66	635	81	52	1	11	145	18	16	6	15	55
XI-A†	556	130	15	81	782	9	1	4	1	15	12	11	5	10	38

* Numbers in this line are coded as follows:
1 = Protestants; 1,685 opinionnaires were sent out; 577 replies received; 34 percent.
2 = Roman Catholics; 434 opinionnaires were sent out; 142 replies received; 33 percent.
3 = Jews; 149 opinionnaires were sent out; 24 replies received; 16 percent.
4 = Selected by the Director, but unclassified with respect to religious faiths; 232 opinionnaires were sent out; 92 replies received; 40 percent.
5 = Combined groups; 2,500 opinionnaires were sent out; 835 replies received; 33 percent.
† Proposition representing the tentative position of the committee.

TABLE 18

SUMMARY OF OPINIONS OF 835 RELIGIOUS LEADERS ON THE ELEVEN PAIRS OF PROPOSITIONS STATED IN THE OPINION-NAIRE INDICATING PERCENTAGE OF EACH MAJOR FAITH GROUP CHOOSING PROPOSITION FROM EACH PAIR REPRESENTING TENTATIVE POSITION OF THE COMMITTEE AND PERCENTAGE CHOOSING PROPOSITION IN EACH PAIR INTENDED TO BE IN OPPOSITION

PROPOSITION	PERCENT CHOOSING PROPOSITION REPRESENTING TENTATIVE POSITION OF THE COMMITTEE					PERCENT CHOOSING PROPOSITION INTENDED TO BE IN OPPOSITION					PERCENT OF REPLIES NOT USABLE				
	1*	2	3	4	5	1	2	3	4	5	1	2	3	4	5
I-A†	95	97	29	89	93	3	1	67	5	5	2	2	4	5	2
II-B†	89	83	58	87	87	8	14	25	5	9	3	3	17	8	4
III-B†	87	75	42	80	83	10	21	50	12	14	3	3	8	8	3
IV-A†	96	90	17	82	91	1	2	54	7	3	3	8	29	12	6
V-B†	94	86	38	85	90	3	4	50	8	5	3	10	12	8	5
VI-B†	79	44	50	73	72	11	38	8	8	15	10	18	42	19	13
VII-A†	90	77	25	84	85	5	11	63	7	8	5	12	12	10	7
VIII-B†	92	83	63	89	89	3	4	33	4	4	5	13	4	7	6
IX-A†	96	86	58	86	92	1	2	21	2	2	3	12	21	12	6
X-B†	83	52	71	72	76	14	37	4	12	17	3	11	25	16	7
XI-A†	96	92	63	88	94	2	1	17	1	2	2	8	21	11	5

* Numbers in this line are coded as follows:
1 = Protestants; 1,685 opinionnaires were sent out; 577 replies received; 34 percent.
2 = Roman Catholics; 434 opinionnaires were sent out; 142 replies received; 33 percent.
3 = Jews; 149 opinionnaires were sent out; 24 replies received; 16 percent.
4 = Selected by the Director, but unclassified with respect to religious faiths; 232 opinionnaires were sent out; 92 replies received; 40 percent.
5 = Combined groups; 2,500 opinionnaires were sent out; 835 replies received; 33 percent.
† Proposition representing the tentative position of the committee.

BIBLIOGRAPHY

Bibliography

This bibliography has been compiled by application of three criteria: (1) publications found most relevant to this study; (2) publications believed to be most useful to others who wish to study the problem; and (3) publications of recent years, and therefore readily accessible. Periodical literature has been omitted except when particularly relevant. The second section contains items illustrative of ways in which schools are dealing with religion.

BOOKS AND STUDIES

ALLEN, HENRY E. (ed.). *Religion in the State University.* 426 South Sixth St., Minneapolis, Minn.: Burgess Publishing Co., 1950. Pp. ix + 123.

A symposium consisting of papers read at a consultative conference for state university administrators and faculty together with national religious leaders, held at the University of Minnesota, Oct. 27–29, 1949. An exploration of the responsibility of state universities for meeting the religious needs of students through the curriculum and counseling. Legal limitations, recent trends, and special problems are considered. Directly relevant to and in general supports the position of the Committee on Religion and Education in its 1953 report.

BACH, MARCUS. *Of Faith and Learning: The Story of the School of Religion at the State University of Iowa.* Iowa City, Iowa: School of Religion, State University of Iowa, 1952. Pp. 261.

A popular narrative of this unique school of religion in a state university with faculty representing the three major faiths.

BERNSTEIN, PHILIP S. *What the Jews Believe.* New York: Farrar, Straus & Young, 1950. Pp. 100.

Suitable for teachers and high school and college students.

BLAU, JOSEPH L. (ed.). *Cornerstones of Religious Freedom in America: Selected Basic Documents, Court Decisions, and Public Statements.* New York: Beacon Press, 1950. Pp. viii + 250.

Useful especially as convenient source of historical documents.

BOWER, WILLIAM CLAYTON. *Moral and Spiritual Values in Education: A Challenge to Every American.* Lexington, Ky.: University of Kentucky Press, 1952. Pp. xv + 214.

A report of the first three years of the Kentucky experiments in developing moral and spiritual values, placed in the historical setting of separation of church and state.

BRADEN, CHARLES S. *The Scriptures of Mankind: An Introduction.* New York: Macmillan Co., 1952. Pp. xiii + 496.

This book is intended to serve as a reading guide for college students in courses dealing with the religions of the world. It stresses historical settings, interpretations, and brief selections from the principal living religions. Useful as a source book for teachers in the public elementary and secondary schools.

BRUBACHER, JOHN S. (ed.). *The Public Schools and Spiritual Values.* Seventh Yearbook of the John Dewey Society. New York: Harper & Bros., 1944. Pp. x + 222.

Written in collaboration by John S. Brubacher, Samuel M. Brownell, John L. Childs, Ruth Cunningham, William H. Kilpatrick, Marion Y. Ostrander, William J. Sanders, and A. L. Threlkeld.

The first significant statement by a group of eminent educators of the responsibility of public schools for developing spiritual values and a defense of a naturalistic approach to spiritual values in the public schools on the assumption that explicit reference to religion is unnecessary and not feasible.

BUTTS, R. FREEMAN. *The American Tradition in Religion and Education.* Boston: Beacon Press, 1950. Pp. xiv + 230.

An analysis and interpretation of the historical documents relating to the separation of church and state and a defense of the thesis that these documents were meant to preclude multiple establishment (use of public funds to support several or all religious bodies) as well as establishment of any one religion.

CHILDS, JOHN L. *Education and Morals: An Experimentalist Philosophy of Education.* New York: Appleton-Century-Crofts, 1950. Pp. xiv + 299.

An analysis and interpretation of the responsibility of education in developing moral values from a naturalistic, "experimentalist" point of view.

COMMITTEE ON RELIGION AND EDUCATION OF THE AMERICAN COUNCIL ON EDUCATION. *The Relation of Religion to Public Education: The Basic Principles.* Washington: American Council on Education, 1947. Pp. vii + 54.

The basic terms of reference for the current (1953) report.

COUNTS, GEORGE S. *Education and American Civilization.* New York: Bureau of Publications, Teachers College, Columbia University, 1952. Pp. xiii + 491.

An excellent section on sources and implications of values, including the Hebraic-Christian ethic.

CUNINGGIM, MERRIMON. *The College Seeks Religion.* New Haven: Yale University Press, 1947. Pp. x + 319.

A study of ways in which the four-year college (excluding teachers colleges, Catholic, Negro, and junior colleges) is meeting the religious needs of students in curricular and extracurricular activities. Finds a trend to greater concern and provision since World War I. Compares public, independent, and church-related colleges, and describes significant programs in a select group of institutions. Relevant to the 1953 report of the Committee on Religion and Education principally in indicating trends.

DAVIS, MARY DABNEY. *Week-Day Religious Instruction.* U.S. Department of the Interior, Office of Education, Pamphlet No. 36. Washington: Government Printing Office, 1933. Pp. 34.

A 1932 survey based on reports from 2,043 cities, indicating that 218 cities in thirty-five states at that time released pupils for religious instruction.

————. *Week-Day Classes in Religious Education: Conducted on Released School Time for Public School Pupils.* U.S. Office of Education, Federal Security Agency, Bulletin 1941, No. 3. Washington: Government Printing Office, 1941. Pp. 66.

A 1940 survey based on reports from 3,790 cities, indicating that 488 cities then had such programs.

DEPARTMENT OF ELEMENTARY SCHOOL PRINCIPALS. *Spiritual Values in the Elementary School: The National Elementary Principal, Bulletin of the Department of Elementary School Principals, National Education Association of the United States; Twenty-sixth Yearbook.* September 1947. Pp. 351.

Descriptions of elementary school practice in defense of the contributions of the public schools to spiritual values.

DRACHER, NORMAN. "The Influence of Sectarianism, Non-Sectarianism, and Secularism upon the Public Schools of Detroit and the University of Michigan, 1837–1900." Doctoral dissertation, University of Michigan, 1951. Pp. 171.

"The study examines the legal structure of the state as it pertained to the relationships of religion and education. The debates and adopted resolutions of the first two constitutional conventions of 1835 and 1850, . . . indicate clearly that the framers of Michigan constitutions carefully provided for separation of church and state.

"The records of the Detroit Board of Education, the University of Michigan, the superintendents of public instruction, as well as other contemporary sources, reveal that educational practices associated with religious aims were often so much more firmly rooted than constitutional restrictions that a religious, often a Protestant, influence continued to prevail in public education.

". . . The public school withstood the powerful pressures of religious groups and succeeded in finding in secularism a formula for survival and growth." [Quoted from Helen F. Spaulding, "Abstracts of Doctoral Dissertations in Religious Education, 1950–1951," *Religious Education,* XLVII (May-June, 1952), 208–31.]

EDUCATIONAL POLICIES COMMISSION OF THE NATIONAL EDUCATION ASSOCIATION OF THE UNITED STATES AND THE AMERICAN ASSOCIATION OF SCHOOL ADMINISTRATORS. *Moral and Spiritual Values in the Public Schools.* Washington: The Commission, 1951. Pp. x + 100.

An authoritative and lucid statement of policy for public education as partner of home and church in developing moral and spiritual values, unequivocally stating that the public schools can and should teach about religion. This report is indispensable to educators, religionists, and laymen concerned with the dilemma of an effective general education and separation of church and state.

ESPY, R. H. *The Religion of College Teachers: The Beliefs, Practices and Religious Preparation of Faculty Members in Church-Related Colleges.* New York: Association Press, 1951. Pp. xxi + 216.

Of interest especially in showing that instructors even in the church-related colleges do not fully sense their responsibility or know how to deal with the facts and implications of religion intrinsic to their fields.

FAIRCHILD, HOXIE N. (ed.). *Religious Perspectives in College Teaching.* New York: Ronald Press, 1952. Pp. x + 460.

This volume contains the pamphlets published earlier serially under the same title by the Edward W. Hazen Foundation. The first chapter deals with problems and principles. The following chapters deal in order with English literature, history, philosophy, classics, music, physical sciences, biology, experimental psychology, sociology and social psychology, anthropology, economics, political science, and the preparation of teachers. Each chapter was written by a scholar in the particular academic discipline. This book presents the most explicit statements currently available of the facts and implications of religion intrinsic to these disciplines and the views of the fourteen authors of their respective attitudes toward the teacher's obligation to deal with them.

FINKELSTEIN, LOUIS. *The Beliefs and Practices of Judaism.* New York: Devin-Adair Co., 1941. Pp. 94.

An authoritative statement by the president of the Jewish Theological Seminary of America, in brief, simple language. An attempt to present the common fundamentals of the different schools of Jewish thought. Suitable for teachers and high school and college students

FITCH, FLORENCE MARY. *One God: The Ways We Worship Him.* New York: Lothrop, Lee & Shepard Co., 1944. Pp. 144.

Intended for teachers and children. Scrupulously fair, accurate, with great insight and appreciation of values; many pictures. Sections devoted to "The Jewish Way," "The Catholic Way," and "The Protestant Way." Endorsed by leading educators and organizations of these faiths.

FLEMING, W. S. *God in Our Public Schools.* 209 Ninth St., Pittsburgh, Pa.: National Reform Association, 1943. Pp. 248.

An argument for the teaching of a nonsectarian religion in the public schools, to aid in character building, in turning back the rising tide of secularism and crime, and in restoring the Biblical truths on which the founding fathers established the nation.

HAY, CLYDE LEMONT. *The Blind Spot in American Public Education.* New York: Macmillan Co., 1950. Pp. xvi + 110.

This book supports the thesis "that a type of religious education can be worked out which will entirely harmonize with the beliefs of Protestants, Catholics, and Jews and which will at the same time be in harmony with the Constitution and the law."

EDWARD W. HAZEN FOUNDATION, and the COMMITTEE ON RELIGION AND EDUCATION OF THE AMERICAN COUNCIL ON EDUCATION. *College Reading and Religion: Being Reports of a Survey of College Reading Materials.* New Haven, Conn.: Yale University Press, 1948. Pp. xi + 345.

Specialists in thirteen fields [history of philosophy, problems of philosophy, psychology, psychiatry, history and philosophy of education, English literature, music, European history, economics, sociology, cultural anthropology, physical sciences, and biological sciences] surveyed the most commonly assigned readings in their respective fields from the point of view of adequacy of treatment of religion.

Donald P. Cottrell, chairman of the committee, concludes: ". . . it is evident that religion is a neglected field of reading and study on the part of college students. The lightness of touch and even ignorance with which intellectual issues having a religious bearing or import are dealt with would seem little less than astonishing when the expansion of scholarship in general is taken into account. Moreover, the hostility to religion revealed in some of the textbooks described becomes perhaps most effective when it is implied or suggested through the aggressive development of a positivistic attitude. . . ."

HENRY, VIRGIL. *The Place of Religion in Public Schools: A Handbook to Guide Communities.* New York: Harper & Bros., 1950. Pp. x + 164.

A doctoral project which is based on the committee's 1947 report; intended to serve as a guide to communities in introducing objective study of religion into the public schools. Discusses content, training of teachers, and development of community understandings.

GAEBELEIN, FRANK E. *Christian Education in a Democracy: The Philosophy and Practice of Christian Education.* New York: Oxford University Press, 1951. Pp. ix + 305.

This book represents an attempt to resolve what the author calls the dilemma of secularism and sectarianism in independent and public education by a nonsectarian Christian orientation.

GAUSS, CHRISTIAN (ed.). *The Teaching of Religion in American Higher Education.* New York: Ronald Press Co., 1951. Pp. viii + 158.

This volume was prepared by a committee sponsored by the National Council on Religion in Higher Education and the Edward W. Hazen Foundation. It deals with the problems of religion and democracy in the United States and gives illustrations of different types of programs in colleges and universities. Supports the position of the Committee on Religion and Education in its 1953 report.

JOHNSON, F. ERNEST (ed.). *American Education and Religion: The Problem of Religion in the Schools.* New York: Harper & Bros., 1952. Pp. ix + 211.

This volume is based on lectures given at the Institute of Religious and Social Studies of the Jewish Theological Seminary of America during the winter of 1950–51. An excellent presentation of the issues by educational and religious leaders.

JOHNSON, GEORGE. *Better Men for Better Times.* Washington: Catholic University of America Press, 1943. Pp. 125.

A concise presentation of the essential objectives of Roman Catholic education with particular reference to the United States. Supports proposition that public school curriculum should include religious references.

INTERNATIONAL COUNCIL OF RELIGIOUS EDUCATION. *Christian Education Today: A Statement of Basic Philosophy.* 206 South Michigan Ave., Chicago 4, Ill.: The Council, 1940. Pp. 40.

Contains sections on "Religion and Public Education" and "Religion in Higher Education." Takes the position that a common core of religious belief can be taught.

KAPLAN, MORDECAI; WILLIAMS, J. PAUL; and KOHN, EUGENE. *The Faith of America: Readings, Songs, and Prayers for the Celebration of American Holidays.* New York: Henry Schuman, 1951. Pp. xxx + 328.

A book intended "to foster faith in American democracy" by the observance of holidays, but omits the religious holidays. Excellent materials provided.

LAUWERYS, J. A., and HANS, N. *The Yearbook of Education* [Education and Morals]. London: Evans Bros., Ltd., 1951. Pp. xii + 674.

Contains contributions from educators from every continent on the general theme of moral education and ways in which different educational systems deal with the problem.

LIGON, ERNEST M. *A Greater Generation.* New York: Macmillan Co., 1950. Pp. xii + 157.

A description of the work of the Union College Character Research Project. Application of psychology to religious education. Its relevance to this report is principally in showing the complexity of character education and religious education.

LIMBERT, PAUL M. (ed.). *College Teaching and Christian Values.* New York: Association Press, 1951. Pp. 187.

Specialists in eight fields (biology, economics, English, geology, history, psychology, and religion) discuss Christian vocation in relation to their respective fields of teaching. Of interest principally to church-related colleges and universities.

MADDEN, WARD. *Religious Values in Education.* New York: Harper & Bros., 1951. Pp. xiii + 203.

The author believes that current discussions of the function of public education in dealing with religion are really debating the validity of supernatural religion without making this fact explicit. He views education as a "creative social act" which he maintains is the "ultimate object of religious devotion." The book is therefore a defense of a nonsectarian religious quality of experience in public education—not a new religion—and he does not think that the public schools can or should study "structured religion."

MOBERLY, SIR WALTER. *The Crisis in the University.* 56 Bloomsbury St., London, England: SCM Press Ltd., 1949. Pp. 316.

A penetrating analysis of higher education in Great Britain and a cogent argument for challenging students with Christianity. In general supports those who believe in teaching a common core of religious belief.

MOEHLMAN, CONRAD H. *The Wall of Separation Between Church and State.* Boston: The Beacon Press, 1951. Pp. xvi + 239.

A defense of the concept of "a high and impregnable wall of separation of church and state" which does not discuss the problem studied by the Committee on Religion and Education in its 1953 report.

NATIONAL EDUCATION ASSOCIATION OF THE UNITED STATES, RESEARCH DIVISION. *The State and Sectarian Education.* Washington: The Association, February 1946. Pp. 44.

Includes a historical introduction and analyzes "the constitutional, statutory, and judicial bases underlying many types of relationship between church and state with respect to education. It provides the basis for further study and discussion in every state."

————. *The Status of Religious Education in the Public Schools.* Washington: The Association, 1949. Pp. 35. (Offset.)

Reviews previous studies and summarizes findings of inquiries sent to 5,100 local superintendents of schools in December 1948, indicating "the type of religious-education program existing in the school system, the number and grade levels of the pupils, the discontinuance of former programs and reasons therefor, and the point of view of the teachers and the community as to the desirability of religious education in the public schools."

NATIONAL PREPARATORY SCHOOL COMMITTEE. *God's Purpose and Our Task in the Schools.* 129 East 52nd St., New York: The Committee, 1951. Pp. 96.

Addresses and papers presented at the national conference on religion in independent schools at Atlantic City, New Jersey, Oct. 19–21, 1950. Supports the view that a common core of religious beliefs should be taught in independent schools.

O'NEILL, J. M. *Religion and Education under the Constitution.* New York: Harper & Bros., 1949. Pp. xii + 338.

An interpretation of the meaning of the First Amendment to the Constitution of the United States. In opposition to interpretations of Butts and Moehlman.

PIEPER, JOSEF, and RASKOP, HEINZ. *What Catholics Believe.* New York: Pantheon Books, 1951. Pp. xiv + 112.

A brief and simple statement of the teachings of the Roman Catholic Church. Suitable for teachers and high school and college students.

Religious Education, Moral and Spiritual Values in the Public Schools: A Symposium. [29 North Pleasant St., Oberlin, Ohio.] *Religious Education,* XLVI (July-August 1951), 195–256.

Fifteen evaluations of the Educational Policies Commission's 1951 report on *Moral and Spiritual Values in the Public Schools.*

SALISBURY, W. SEWARD. *Religion in America.* New York: Oxford Book Co., 1951. Pp. iv + 60.

A brief factual treatment of religion in America.

————. *The Organization and Practice of Religion in a Small City.* Oswego, N.Y.: Ontario Press, not dated. Pp. 40.

This pamphlet is a description of the churches of Oswego, New York, which "arose out of an attempt to make the study of religion [in a course in sociology in the New York State Teachers College at Oswego] more meaningful and real for the students. . . . The students made the initial investigations as part of their field work. . . ."

SPAULDING, HELEN F. "Abstracts of Doctoral Dissertations in Religious Education, 1950–1951," *Religious Education,* XLVII (May-June 1952), 208–31.

Abstracts of thirty-three doctoral dissertations on various aspects of religious education completed in 1950–51, indicating institutions, sponsoring committees, problems, procedures, and principal findings and conclusions. Those of particular relevance to objective study of religion have been listed in alphabetical order in this bibliography.

STOKES, ANSON PHELPS. *Church and State in the United States.* New York: Harper & Bros., 1950. 3 vols. Pp. lxix + 2777.

A monumental historical survey and source book including many documents and interpretation of events contributing to the growth of religious freedom. Takes the position that the intent and effect has been a friendly constitutional separation of church and state. Includes much on the status of the church and synagogue, and religious bodies.

TEAD, ORDWAY. *Trustees-Teachers-Students: Their Role in Higher Education.* Salt Lake City: University of Utah Press, 1951. Pp. 120.

Contains sections on the role of religion in higher education, which support the 1953 position of the Committee on Religion and Education.

THAYER, V. T. *The Attack Upon the American Secular School.* Boston: Beacon Press, 1951. Pp. x + 257.

An argument for the "secularism" of the public school on the grounds that it is not an "ism" or a "false" philosophy, but rather "a term which designates an effort to arrive at a still broader base of common agreement in a heterogeneous population." The author believes that objective study of religion is justifiable and legal in the public schools, but takes sharp issue with what he believes to be the implications of the 1947 report of the Committee on Religion and Education.

VAN DUSEN, HENRY P. *God in Education: A Tract for Our Times.* New York: Charles Scribner's Sons, 1951. Pp. 128.

What the author is aiming at is a philosophy of education on all levels which rests firmly on the conception of the unity of truth and of human experience. The focus of attention is chiefly higher education. The author deplores the extreme secularization of elementary and secondary education. The reader gains the impression that he would like to see public as well as private education adopt a definitely theistic outlook but that as a genuine liberal he wants to preserve the freedom of the mind from pressures of indoctrination.

WARREN, HAROLD C. "Changing Conceptions in the Religious Elements in Early American School Readers." Doctoral dissertation, University of Pittsburgh, 1951. Pp. 358.

"The author undertook to list, analyze, and interpret instances [of appearance of specific ideas] of a religious nature within readers from 1690 to 1880, limiting consideration to books intended for children of primary age . . . most widely used and influential.

[Findings reveal trends in the culture] "All of this was accelerated by the rise of sectarianism in America, with loss of authority by the church and assumption of authority by the state." [Quoted from Helen F. Spaulding, "Abstracts of Doctoral Dissertations in Religious Education, 1950–1951," *Religious Education,* XLVII (May-June 1952), 208–31.]

WILDER, AMOS N. (ed). *Liberal Learning and Religion: A Vital Discussion of Major Issues Confronting the Universities Where There Is Serious Concern for Religion.* New York: Harper & Bros., 1951. Pp. xi + 338.

Contributions of fifteen scholars. Deals with problems of religious values, teaching religion, and academic freedom in higher education in general, not public education in particular.

WILLIAMS, J. PAUL. *The New Education and Religion: The Role of Religion in Shaping American Destiny.* New York: Association Press, 1946. Pp. x + 198.

A defense of the thesis that the teaching of religion (not sectarianism) must be returned to the schools and a discussion of ways in which "American public and private institutions can, without compromising religious freedom, provide a more adequate education in religion." Dr. Williams devotes more than half of his book to "The Possible Solutions" and "Toward a Better Education."

————. *What Americans Believe and How They Worship.* New York: Harper & Bros., 1952. Pp. x + 400.

An attempt "to set down the facts and let them speak for themselves" in the sense that "Catholics assert," "Methodists believe," "Mormons teach," etc. The following religious groups are included: Catholics, Lutherans, Episcopalians, Presbyterians, Congregationalists, Unitarians, Baptists, Disciples, Quakers, Methodists, Jews, and some of the newer groups, including Pentecostals, Adventists, and Mormons. A source book for the teacher who wishes to understand the role of religion in American life. The concluding chapter on "The Role of Religion in Shaping American Destiny" presents some of the basic issues.

WILSON, KARL K. "Historical Survey of Religious Content of American Geography Textbooks from 1784 to 1895." Doctoral dissertation, University of Pittsburgh, 1951. Pp. 254.

"There was a steady decline in the amount of space given to religious content as the principle of separation of church and state became more fully accepted by the people. History was often included in the early geography textbooks. The space allotted to each religion usually compared favorably with the number of its adherents." [Quoted from Helen F. Spaulding, "Abstracts of Doctoral Dissertations in Religious Education, 1950–1951," *Religious Education,* XLVII (May-June 1952), 208–31.]

WROTEN, JAMES DAUSEY, JR. "Experimental Development of a College Course on the Church and Society." Doctoral dissertation, Columbia University, 1951. Pp. 212.

"The purpose of the project was to discover the functional possibilities of the church in society. A college course called 'The Church and Society' was developed . . . at Millsaps College. . . . Twenty-three students chose to make the experiment with the author.

"The author and students chose to use the democratic discussion method. . . .

"The class made a questionnaire [on issues—Race Problems, Crime, Alcohol, Community Relations, Leisure] to be taken to the churches throughout Mississippi, seeking to determine what the church was doing in society. Comparisons were made between what the class thought the church should do in society and what they found the church doing. From this came suggestions for improvement of the churches' role in society. Some experiments for improvements were carried on by members of the class who were ministers of churches.

". . . The democratic process makes possible the formation and development of ideas and attitudes to a degree that cannot be reached in the lecture type course." [Quoted from Helen F. Spaulding, "Abstracts of Doctoral Dissertations in Religious Education, 1950–1951," *Religious Education,* XLVII (May-June 1952), 208–31.]

YALE UNIVERSITY DIVINITY SCHOOL. *Religion in State Teachers Colleges.* New Haven: Yale University Divinity School, 1952. Pp. 39.

A report of a national study conference on "Religion in the State Teachers Colleges" held at Yale University Divinity School, Dec. 15–17, 1951. Includes summary reports of study-workshops on: legal problems; religious courses; religious activities; relation of religion to other disciplines; chapel, worship at local churches; moral and spiritual values in public schools; solving ethical and social problems through resources of religion; and religious counseling. Of special significance is the digest of an address by Prof. Clarence Shedd on "Some Proposals for Religion in State Teachers Colleges."

REPORTS AND COURSES OF STUDY

AGREED SYLLABUSES OF RELIGIOUS INSTRUCTION

The following illustrate the solution of the problem of the place to give religion in tax-supported education in England under the Education Act of 1944. Of particular relevance to the proposal to teach a common core of religious belief.

EXETER [England] EDUCATION COMMITTEE. *Agreed Syllabus of Religious Instruction.* 33 St. David's Hill, Exeter, England: City Education Offices, 1948. Pp. 40.

LONDON [England] COUNTY COUNCIL. *The London Syllabus of Religious Education.* London: The Council, 1947. Pp. 168.

MIDDLESEX COUNTY [England]. *Middlesex County Council Agreed Syllabus of Religious Instruction.* 10, Great George St., Westminster, London, S.W.1: Middlesex County Council, 1948. Pp. 287 + (20).

SURREY COUNTY COUNCIL. *Syllabus of Religious Instruction.* Guilford, Surrey County, England: Biddles, Ltd., 1947. Pp. 110.

BALTIMORE CITY PUBLIC SCHOOLS. *Better Intercultural Relations.* Baltimore, Md.: Office of the Superintendent, Baltimore City Public Schools, 1948. Pp. 34.

An outline of facts, their relevance to the curriculum, activities, and readings. Section on "Different Religious Faiths."

————. *Resource Units for World History.* Baltimore, Md.: Office of the Superintendent, Baltimore City Public Schools, 1948. Pp. iv + 79. (Mimeographed.)

Contains unit on "The Fertile Crescent," which deals extensively with religion, and a unit on "Religion During the Middle Ages." An excellent example of objective treatment of religion.

BOARD OF EDUCATION OF BALTIMORE COUNTY, MARYLAND. *Religion: Man's Search for God.* Towson 4, Md.: The Board, 1948. Pp. 26. (Mimeographed.)

Unit Four, tenth grade, World History, outline on "Religion: Man's Search for God."

BIRMINGHAM SUNDAY SCHOOL COUNCIL. *Annual Report, 1951.* 511 Title Guarantee Building, Birmingham, Ala.: The Council, *n.d.*

Includes census of school children attending Sunday School which is taken annually with the cooperation of the schools for a four-week period prior to Easter.

BOSTON PUBLIC SCHOOLS. *A Handbook on the Principles of American Democracy.* Boston: School Committee, 1948. Pp. 93.

Contains discussion of religious freedom and other topics related to religion.

GEORGE NIXON BRADY SCHOOL. *Brady School Plan for Character and Citizenship Training.* 2920 Joy Road, Detroit 6, Mich.: The School. Pp. 76.

A description of a character and citizenship program in a public elementary school which has given rise to controversy on the grounds that it is religious education, which investigating committees have denied. Of particular relevance to the legitimate place of religious observances in the public schools.

CHARLOTTE PUBLIC SCHOOLS. *Have You Heard These Facts about Bible in the Schools?* Charlotte, N.C.: Executive Committee for Bible Teaching in the Public Schools in Charlotte, North Carolina, 1949. Pp. 15.

Describes the program of Bible teaching in the regular curriculum. (Elective.)

COMMISSION ON WEEKDAY RELIGIOUS EDUCATION, DEPARTMENT OF CHRISTIAN EDUCATION, COUNCIL OF CHURCHES OF CHRIST OF ALLEGHENY COUNTY. *Weekday Religious Education Workbooks.* 230 Oliver Ave., Pittsburgh 22, Pa.: The Commission.

For high school students and instructors. Ten courses in a set. Each course a complete unit. Sample copies free. For use in released time program.

Course A: How the Bible Grew (seventh grade)
Course B: Bible Lands, Peoples, and Customs (eighth grade)

Course I: The Life of Christ (ninth grade, first semester)

Course II: The Teachings of Jesus (ninth grade, second semester)

Course III: Old Testament Biography and History (tenth grade, first semester)

Course IV: Old Testament Biography and History (tenth grade, second semester)

Course V: New Testament Biography and History (eleventh grade, first semester)

Course VI: New Testament Biography and History (eleventh grade, second semester)

Course VII: The History of the Christian Church (twelfth grade, first semester)

Course VIII: The Church in America (twelfth grade, second semester)

DALLAS HIGH SCHOOLS. *Bible Study Course—Old Testament.* Dallas, Texas: Dallas Independent School District, 1949. Pp. xiv + 96.

Bulletin No. 150. Authorized by the Board of Education, for study out of school and one-half unit of credit toward high school graduation.

————. *Bible Study Course—New Testament.* Dallas, Texas: Dallas Independent School District, 1950. Pp. xiv + 121.

Bulletin No. 170. Authorized by the Board of Education, for study out of school and one-half unit of credit toward high school graduation.

DETROIT PUBLIC SCHOOLS. *A Pupil Manual and Study Guide in Elementary Social Studies.* Detroit: Public Schools, 1948. Pp. v + 118. (Sixth Grade.)

Under the title: "How People Live Together" units on the following are included: "The Story of Education," "The Story of Government," "The Story of Religion," "The Story of Science and Scientists," and "The Story of the Arts." Includes objective treatment of all religions.

FLINN, VIRGIL L. *Religious Education in the Public Schools.* Charleston, W. Va. Board of Education of the County of Kanawha, 1947. Pp. 44. (Mimeographed.)

A report to the board of education, including legal factors and alternatives to be considered in adopting a policy.

GLENDALE UNIFIED SCHOOL DISTRICT. *Outline of Course in Medieval History.* Glendale, Calif.: Glendale Unified School District. Pp. 13. (Mimeographed.)

Outline of course in medieval history indicating the inclusion of topics on religion and religious institutions.

————. *Curriculum Guide for Released Time Program.* Glendale, Calif.: Glendale Unified School District. Pp. 17. (Mimeographed and bound.)

A suggested program for pupils who remain at school during the period of released time for religious instruction. A guidance and activity program in character education.

HARTFORD PUBLIC SCHOOLS. *Carrying American Ideals into Action.* Hartford, Conn.: Public Schools, 1944. Pp. 54. (Mimeographed.)

A report of the Intertown Committee on Character Education representing the schools of greater Hartford. Emphasis upon self-discipline, mutual understanding, and spiritual purpose. Contains a section on "The Contribution of Religion."

HAWAII DEPARTMENT OF PUBLIC INSTRUCTION. *Moral and Ethical Values in the Public Schools of Hawaii.* Honolulu, T.H.: The Department, 1949. Pp. 55. |Illustrated.)

An excellent statement of the operational principles of development of values in the quality of living and working in the public schools from a secular point of view. Superbly illustrated.

HIGHLAND PARK PUBLIC SCHOOLS. *Devotionals.* 3610 Cornell, Dallas 5, Texas: Highland Park Public Schools, 1950. Pp. 101. (Mimeographed and bound.)

Materials developed for use in devotional opening exercises in the Highland Park Public Schools.

HOUSTON PUBLIC SCHOOLS. *Moral and Spiritual Values Stressed in the Houston Public Schools.* Houston, Texas: Houston Public Schools, 1951. Pp. 35. (Mimeographed.)

Released for criticism and comment as Curriculum Bulletin 51CBM9.

HUNT, HEROLD C. *Satisfying Spiritual and Aesthetic Needs.* 229 North LaSalle St., Chicago 1, Ill.: Board of Education. Pp. 10. (Mimeographed.)

A statement of philosophy by General Superintendent Hunt and a statement of aims and pupil behavior objectives by a Committee on Spiritual and Aesthetic Needs.

IDAHO STATE BOARD OF EDUCATION. *List of Selections from the Standard American Version of the Bible for Daily Reading in the Public Schools.* Boise, Idaho: State Department of Education. Pp. 15. (Mimeographed.)

Selections listed under "Prose and Poetry," "Great Orations and Addresses," "Great Prayers," "Great Songs and Lyrics," "Words of

Wisdom, Promise, and Prophecy," "Life of Jesus," "Miracles, Old Testament," "Parables," "Letters, in Parts," and "Narrative."

INTERNATIONAL COUNCIL OF RELIGIOUS EDUCATION, DEPARTMENT OF WEEKDAY RELIGIOUS EDUCATION. *Remember the Weekday to Teach Religion Thereon.* 203 North Wabash Ave., Chicago 1, Ill.: The Council. (Leaflet.)

Brief answers to questions commonly asked about weekday church schools.

KENT STATE UNIVERSITY. *Syllabus for Graduate Course on Moral and Spiritual Values in the Public Schools.* Kent, Ohio: The University, 1952. Pp. 8. (Mimeographed.)

Contains a unit on "Religion in the Public Schools."

KENTUCKY DEPARTMENT OF EDUCATION. "Moral and Spiritual Values in Education," *Educational Bulletin,* XVIII (October 1950), 731–911.

A report on the second workshop on discovering: (1) how to improve human relations; and (2) how to make the curriculum meaningful in life. This is part of a state-wide program now in its fourth year.

———. "Moral and Spiritual Values in Public Schools," *Educational Bulletin,* XIX (February 1952), 1159–1218.

Digest of lectures by Dr. William Heard Kilpatrick and reports on workshops held in certain teacher-training institutions during the summer of 1951. This is part of a state-wide program now in its fourth year.

KENTUCKY STATE PROGRAM OF MORAL AND SPIRITUAL EDUCATION.

Write Mr. J. Mansir Tydings, Director of Moral and Spiritual Education, 1275 Starks Bldg., Louisville, Ky., for information on the Kentucky Program of Moral and Spiritual Education. See also William Clayton Bower, *Moral and Spiritual Values in Education,* listed above.

WILLIAM J. KERBY FOUNDATION. [Leaflets on] *Spiritual Foundations of American Democracy.* Washington: Catholic University of America William J. Kerby Foundation.

These leaflets are designed to implement the conception of Dr. Kerby that "Democracy is primarily social, moral, and spiritual, and secondarily political."

LOS ANGELES CITY SCHOOL DISTRICTS. *Moral and Spiritual Values in Education.* Los Angeles: Curriculum Division, Los Angeles City School Districts, 1947. Pp. 54. (Mimeographed.)

Progress reports from junior and senior high schools, including anecdotal records of changes in behavior.

———. *The Faith of Youth.* Los Angeles: Curriculum Division, Los Angeles City School Districts, 1950. Pp. 14. (Mimeographed.)

Report of a survey of high school seniors' attitudes about religion.

———. *Practicing the Democratic Way in School.* Los Angeles: Curriculum Division, Los Angeles City School Districts, 1950. Pp. ix + 64. (Mimeographed.)

A teacher's guide. "An attempt to show in simple, workable form the kind of spirit which prevails and the kind of experiences which take place in a classroom in which democratic practices prevail."

———. *The E in UNESCO.* Los Angeles: Curriculum Division, Los Angeles City School Districts, 1951. Pp. 96.

Suggestions for teachers on techniques, materials, and information. Contains helpful information on brotherhood and human rights.

LOS ANGELES COUNTY PUBLIC SCHOOLS. *Cooperative Project in Human Relations: Summary Analysis.* Los Angeles: Office of the County Superintendent, Los Angeles County Public Schools. Pp. 18. (Mimeographed.)

A cooperative program of "Work Study Groups," "Pilot Projects," and "Action-Research." Not directly relevant to religion, but indirectly helpful on dynamics of human relations involved in objective study of religion.

MAINE STATE DEPARTMENT OF EDUCATION. *Character Education.* [*See bulletins listed below.*] Augusta: State Department of Education.

Character Education and Accredited Bible Study in the State of Maine: Objectives, Regulations, Course of Study. Bulletin Number Nine, 1947. Pp. 67.

Heroic Living. 1942. Pp. 24.

Leaders of World Religions. 1945. Pp. 8.

Character Education Through the Fine Arts and Sports. 1948. Pp. 17. (Mimeographed.)

Suggested Character Education Course Outlines for Grades 6, 7, 8 [Released Time]. 1951. Pp. 28 (Mimeographed.)

Top of the Morning—And the Rest of the Day (Suggested Materials for Morning Devotionals). 1952. Pp. 11. (Mimeographed.)

Report of the Committee to Study the Advisability of a More Coordinated Effort in the Field of Character Education in the Schools of the State. 1952. Pp. 21. (Mimeographed.)

MARYLAND STATE DEPARTMENT OF EDUCATION. *Report of the Third Annual Maryland Educational Conference.* Baltimore 2, Md.: Maryland State Department of Education, 1950. Pp. 219.

Contains section (pp. 53–79) on developing ethical, moral, and spiritual values in terms of criteria for evaluation of practices. Not directly relevant to religion, but indirectly helpful on how to evaluate experience in objective study of religion.

MONTANA STATE BOARD OF EDUCATION. *Bible History.* Helena, Mont.: Superintendent of Public Instruction, 1942. Pp. 58. (Mimeographed and bound.)

Prepared for use in Michigan (no longer in use there) and published in Montana by permission of the Michigan Education Association. Syllabus II—New Testament. (Presumably Syllabus I is on the Old Testament.)

Taught outside of school hours in the various churches and credit up to one point toward high school graduation is allowed by certain communities.

NASHVILLE PUBLIC SCHOOLS. *Going Our Way.* Nashville, Tenn.: Office of the Superintendent, Public Schools, 1945. (Mimeographed.)

Four publications: one for grades one and two; one for grades three and four; one for grades five and six; and one for grades seven through twelve. The one for grades three and four is entitled *Going Our Way* and is a 164-page volume (mimeographed). The objective is character education. Much use of religious materials.

NATIONAL ASSOCIATION OF CHRISTIAN SCHOOLS. Various publications. 542 South Dearborn St., Chicago 5, Ill.

Publishes newsletters and leaflets, designed to promote Christian education in church day schools.

NEW YORK STATE PROGRAM OF MORAL AND SPIRITUAL EDUCATION.

Write Dr. A. K. Getman, The State Education Department, Albany 1, N.Y., for literature on program of moral and spiritual education now in preparation.

NORTH CAROLINA EDUCATION ASSOCIATION. *Suggested Twelve-Year Program of Biblical Education for the Public Schools of North Carolina.* Bulletin of the Bible Department of the North Carolina Education Association. Raleigh, N.C.: The Association. Pp. 42. (Mimeographed.)

Course outline by grades for teaching the Bible in the public schools of North Carolina.

NOTT TERRACE HIGH SCHOOL. *Man's Search for Ideals*. Schenectady, N.Y.: Superintendent of Schools. Pp. 5. (Mimeographed.)
Unit in history dealing with world's religions.

OAKLAND PUBLIC SCHOOLS. *Report of Committee on Moral and Spiritual Values in the Oakland Public Schools*. Oakland, Calif.: Office of the Superintendent, Public Schools. Pp. 29. (Mimeographed.)
Includes basic principles, specific recommendations, and suggested readings.

ST. PAUL, MINNESOTA, COUNCIL OF HUMAN RELATIONS. *Sharing the December Holidays*. St. Paul, Minn.: Office of the Superintendent, Public Schools. Pp. 36. (Mimeographed.)
Contains sections on "Historical and Cultural Background of Hanukkah and Christmas," "Problems That Arise," "Suggested Types of Programs," "Music for December Holidays," "Art-Decorations and Things to Do," and "Holiday Book List."

SAN DIEGO CITY SCHOOLS. *Spiritual Values*. San Diego, Calif.: Office of the Superintendent, San Diego City Schools, 1948. Pp. 111.
Summarizing present practices and suggesting activities for the development of spiritual values in education. Many illustrations of principles and procedures.

SCHOOL SUPERINTENDENTS OF CITIES IN THE UNITED STATES AND CANADA WITH POPULATION OVER 200,000. *An Education Platform for the Public Schools*. Chicago, Ill.: School Superintendents, Educational Division, Field Enterprises, Inc., 1952.
Contains statements on the function of the public schools in developing moral and spiritual values and on dealing with controversial issues.

SEATTLE PUBLIC SCHOOLS. *Spiritual Growth Through Reading*. Seattle, Wash.: Office of the Superintendent, Public Schools, 1948. Pp. 12. (Mimeographed.)
A list of books designed to promote the spiritual insight and religious understanding of children.

SPRINGFIELD PUBLIC SCHOOLS. *The Contributions of Religions to Present Democratic Procedures*. Springfield, Mass.: Office of the Superintendent, Public Schools. Pp. 18. (Mimeographed.)
Outline of unit for use in the eighth grade. Objective treatment of all religions of the world.

WELLESLEY SENIOR HIGH SCHOOL. *Devotionals Program at the High School*. Wellesley, Mass.: Senior High School. Pp. 4. (Typed.)
A brief description of the Devotionals Program at the Wellesley, Mass., Senior High School.

AMERICAN COUNCIL ON EDUCATION

Arthur S. Adams, *President*

The American Council on Education is a *council* of national educational associations; organizations having related interests; approved universities, colleges, teachers colleges, junior colleges, technological schools, and selected private secondary schools; state departments of education; city school systems and private school systems; selected educational departments of business and industrial companies; voluntary associations of higher education in the states; and large public libraries. It is a center of cooperation and coordination whose influence has been apparent in the shaping of American educational policies and the formulation of educational practices during the last thirty-four years.

Date Due

Due	Returned	Due	Returned
JAN 0 5 1988	DEC 1 2 1987		
MAY 25 1991	MAY 21 1991		